Alain Prost
The science of racing

Alain Prost
The science of racing

by
Pierre Ménard & Jacques Vassal

Car profiles
Pierre Ménard

Photographs
LAT (unless stated otherwise)

Translated from french by
Eric Silbermann

Design
Cyril Davillerd

Cover
Cyril Davillerd, Sabrina Favre

Layout
Cyril Davillerd, Désirée Ianovici

Contents

Alain_PROST

Chapter 1
1900-1955
Deepest France

Nestling close to Saint-Etienne, Saint-Chamond is buried in deepest France, a hardworking industrial and business town, situated amongst forests, hills, mines and steelworks. It was part of a France that had been built over the centuries, block by block, fashioned by the church and the republic and by original popular traditions too.

The first sign of a town on the site of Saint-Chamond is a stone which, according to its inscription, dates back to the reign of the Emperor Augustus, in 22 BC. But it was not until the seventh century AD that Saint-Ennemond, the Bishop of Lyon came to evangelise the area and the village known in Latin as Sancti-Annemundi became Saint-Chamond. The Catholic religion made its mark on local history over the subsequent centuries with Lord Mechior Mitte de Chevrieres founding in 1634 the college of Saint-Jean Baptiste run by twelve Canons. The Convent of Minimes was founded in 1622 and bought by the commune in 1792 it later became the town hall.

Today, Saint-Chamond has a population of 40,000, well used to taking in workers from foreign lands, notably Armenians, who even have their own association and church in the town and, more recently, the Vietnamese. Situated between Lyon and Saint-Etienne, it followed their development as an industrial town, with coal and steel always playing a key economic role. In the Sixties, the population had already reached 200,000 and most of them made their living in the foundries and steel works which spat out smoke and sparks and the very important Manufacture d'Armes et Cycles (Manufacturer of Arms and Cycles.) It was a tough life, especially as the climate was less than welcoming. Hardly a place to sing about, but the town did produce a well known singer, Bernard Lavilliers, who penned this less than flattering description of his home town:

On n'est pas d'un pays mais on est d'une ville
Où la rue artérielle limite le décor
Les cheminées d'usine hululent à la mort
*La lampe du gardien rigole de mon style...**

However, Saint-Chamond offers a more bucolic vista than its next door neighbour, with woods and water and streams and it skirts what is today the nature reserve of the Pilat region, a veritable paradise for ramblers and cyclists. But the old Gillet-Thaon dyeing plant which dates back to 1876 and the huge 103 metre high chimney of the Giat Industries factory with an even earlier heritage dating from 1863 bear testament to past labours as do the remains of old slag heaps left over from the last mine at Clos Marquet which closed in 1950.

Back in the Fifties, traditional industry still flourished in Saint-Chamond, but there was often a high price to pay: in August 1952, six workmen at the Gillet factory died of hydrogen sulphide poisoning. But the dyeing plant, the Marine Forges and Steelworks and the Creusot-Loire factory held firm, to such an extent that, in order to meet the needs of these industries, the Piney dam was built as the old Rive dam's water level was too low. In 1954 the first "expressway" was built, linking Saint-Chamond with Saint-Etienne around ten kilometres away. This major project was the brainchild of the Mayor, Antoine Pinay, who had also been President of the Regional Council since 1949. Born in 1891, he served the fourth republic as President of the Council and Minister under Vincent Auriol in 1952 then in the fifth republic as Charles de Gaulle's Finance Minister. In 1958, he was seen as the "father of the new franc" and known as the "man with the round hat." He is still remembered today for his long political career. He was mayor of Saint-Chamond for the first time from 12 May 1929 to 20 August 1944 and re-elected on 19 October 1947 and was then re-elected time after time,

● **1**_The Stephanois and Lyon areas and their roads as seen on the French Atlas (taken from Reader's Digest) at the end of the Sixties. Not many motorways in those days, although one can see a rare section from Saint-Chamond to Rive-de-Gier!

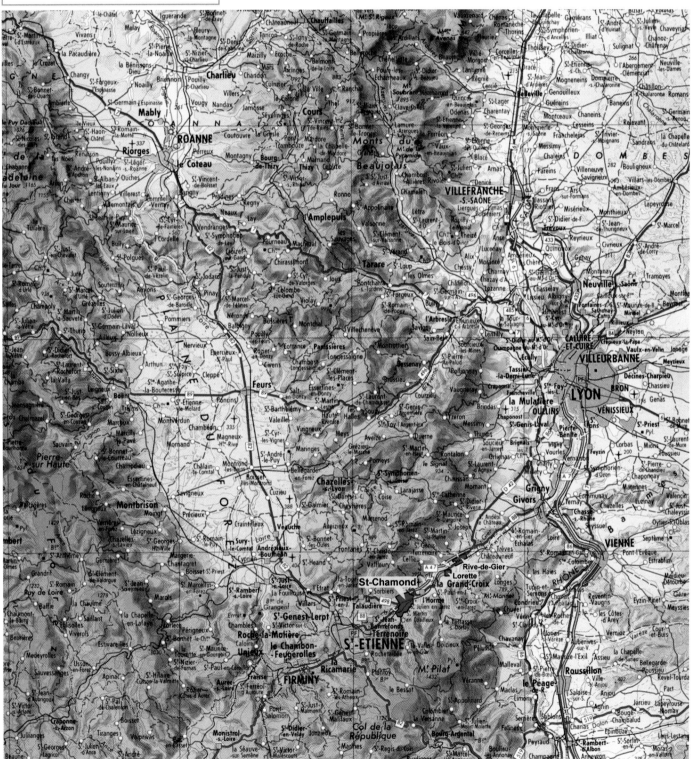

operating a very conservative policy, until 20 March 1977! Nearly 45 years heading up the same municipality: it was a record duly celebrated by the citizens of his town in 1991 and he went on to live past his centenary.

One would think that the countryside and climate of the area plays its part in maintaining the fitness of its inhabitants and indeed, sport has always been a strong point in Saint-Chamond. Especially football with the local Sporting Club, set up in 1911, often beating its nearby rivals. Those with long memories still recall a match in 1936 at the Chaleassiere stadium against the Saint Stephane team. Tensions ran high and the referee had to ask the crowd to make less noise! Therefore, the fact that Alain Prost's career began on the football pitch should come as no surprise. But the folk of Saint-Chamond also excelled in other disciplines, like skiing and ice skating with winter games organised at the Grand' Grange from 1911. Running was also popular and Antoine Vincendon, a member of the C.O.S.C. club became the French 1500 metres champion in 1954. Cycling featured as well, with another local man, René Meunier taking the individual track speed title in 1955, the year of Alain Prost's birth. Much later, the Formula 1 World Champion would also develop a passion for road racing.

While the bicycle figured large in both Saint-Chamond and Saint-Etienne, the region also had long established links with motorised sports. Even as far back as 2 June 1909, the "Velodrome on the Corner" as it was known, organised the first Cycling and Motorcycling Championship. On the car side, the local topography and the twisty roads of the area mean that rallying and hillclimbs are particularly popular. A few years after the war, the difficult Planfoy hillclimb, a few kilometres to the south of Saint-Etienne, attracted the best regional and sometimes even national specialists, who raced in front of a large and enthusiastic crowd. The drivers were divided into Road Car, GT, Sport and single-seater categories. Sadly, in the Fifties, a tragic accident claimed the life of Colonel Heurtaux from Lyon, who crossed the line to win, only to lose control of his Jaguar C type, hitting a post and dying on impact. Partly because of this accident, but also because of stricter safety laws imposed after the catastrophe in the 1955 Le Mans 24 Hours, the Planfoy hillclimb, along with several other events in France were permanently scrubbed. However, rallying continued to grow, including as far as the story of Alain Prost is concerned, the Forez event, which will feature later. Several other rallies came through the area, especially the exclusive Lyon – Charbonnieres,

often run in very difficult weather with rain snow and fog and much of it run at night. On top of that, there were the link sections of the Monte Carlo Rally and sometimes the Tour de France would also pass through Forez.

However, there are no race tracks in Forez, nor were there in the 50s and 60s and amateur racers and race fans had to travel further afield to satisfy their thirst for speed. At Clermont-Ferrand, about 150 kilometres from Saint-Chamond, there was the magnificent Charade circuit, designed on advice from local racer, Louis Rosier and built in 1958. Sadly, Rosier, who had raced with Talbot-Lago, then for Maserati and Ferrari in Formula 1, was killed at Montlhery in October 1956. He never saw his dream become reality. The Charade circuit measured 8.055 kilometres and was technically challenging, earning it the nickname of the "little Nurburgring." With its impressive drops and climbs, especially the Gravenoire descent and the edge of the track lined with stones which threatened to puncture any wayward wheels, it was a real test of man and machine. The races were thrilling for spectators, set against a magnificent backdrop and the viewing areas affording a panoramic view of the circuit. Charade first staged the French Motorcycle Grands Prix and the Trophees d'Auvergne for Sport, GT and Formula Junior cars. Then came Formula 3 and Formula 2 in the shape of the French Grand Prix and French Trophy. The crowning glory for the Automobile Club d'Auvergne and its president, Jean Auchatraire, was the staging of several Formula 1 Grands Prix in 1965, '69, '70 and '72.

French motor sport had been boosted on an international level. After the efforts of craftsmen like Jean Redele (Alpine-Renault) and René Bonnet, (first with the Panhard-engined DB, then the Renault-engined René Bonnet) and then in 1965, with Matra which had taken over René Bonnet. Matra's first international win came in the Formula 3 Coupe de Vitesse at Reims and this opened the way to Formula 2 and Formula 1 for the military aerospace company. It also entered the world of endurance racing, helping to launch a new generation of French drivers who would enjoy great success on the world stage: Jean-Pierre Beltoise, who had taken that famous win at Reims, Henri Pescarolo and Johnny Servoz-Gavin, all three making it into Formula 1. Then came François Cevert who, having joined Tyrrell in 1970, seemed to be on course to become the first French World Champion. Sadly, this hope was cut short when he was killed in a terrible accident in practice for the United States Grand Prix in October 1973.

For various reasons, other French drivers never got the Formula 1 careers their brilliance deserved. Among the older clan in the Fifties, neither Louis Rosier nor Jean Behra, nor Robert Manzon, although worthy competitors, ever won a World Championship race. Maurice Trintignant won two, both at Monaco, but was never a title contender. Jo Schlesser stagnated in Formula 2 for a long time and made it to Formula 1 only to lose his life in his very first race with Honda in 1968. After struggling with the Matra MS 120, Jean-Pierre Beltoise found refuge with BRM. He took one, but only one, majestic win in Monaco in 1972. Henri Pescarolo was no more successful than Beltoise in the Matra and moved on to March, BRM, Iso-Ford and Surtees, with just a few runner-up places to his name. The feisty Jean-Pierre Jarier raced for March, Shadow, ATS, Ligier, Lotus, Osella and Tyrrell. He often led grands prix, but not when he passed the flag.

Jean-Pierre Jabouille's career in Formula 1 saw him leave Renault for Ligier just before being sidelined after an accident. Then came Didier Pironi and in 1982 with Ferrari, it seemed he might become the first French World Champion, but a very serious accident in practice for the German Grand Prix put an end to that. Jacques Laffite was a serious contender in 1979 and 1981, but he never made it. These drivers paved the way for what was to be the exceptional career of Alain Prost... ■

● **2**_Buried deep in the Massif du Forez, the town of Saint-Chamond, pictured in the Eighties.
(Saint-Chamond town hall archive)

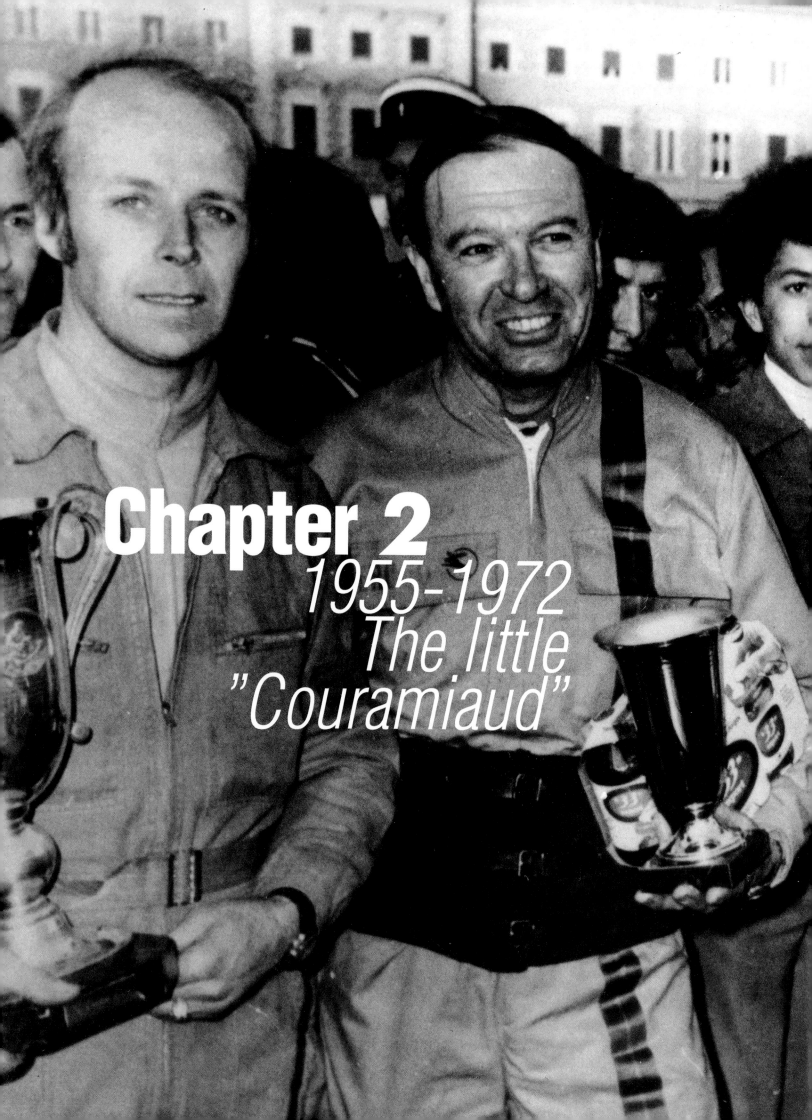

Chapter 2
1955-1972
The little "Couramiaud"

There is nothing striking about the house at 21 Rue Dugas-Montbel near the Saint-Chamond station, as far as passers by are concerned, but for the fact it is home to a small family business designing and making small items of furniture. The workshop is in the basement, the offices on the ground floor and the living area upstairs. Set up by André Prost, the "Toutube" company started in the Fifties making items from welded tubes, such as cycle racks. The business prospered and the range increased to encompass hi-fi stands and kitchen items. By the Sixties, it was flourishing and employed around twenty people over and above the Prost family themselves. André, the father, looked after the assembly, the mother, Marie-Rose, did the upholstery and André, the paternal grandfather saw to the accounts. Then, the two sons came to help in the basement workshop, not in order to earn a bit of cash, but because in the Prost family, the work ethic was seen as a moral and incontrovertible necessity. The children were expected to understand the notion of work and his value and this formed much of the basis of their education. There was very little free time to offset the workload. Lunch never lasted much more than ten minutes and Marie-Rose would often cover the hi-fi furniture in the kitchen to save time. *"My father was very calm,"* recalls Alain Prost today. *"He did not talk much, except to give out and my mother was, and still is, permanently wired up to 100,000 volts. She cannot stop and always has to move forward and in this respect, it's true that I am like her. My mother would eat standing up, in three minutes and that's still the case today! Everyone was always in a hurry so as not to waste time."*

The Prost family did not waste time in futile leisure pursuits. They had no interest in sport and hardly ever went to the cinema. On Sunday, the only day off in the week, they would usually go and lunch with friends or cousins. The only concession to pleasure was digging for mushrooms while André hunted thrushes. He often took little Alain along who was delighted to fill his lungs with the early morning air of the woods in neighbouring Dombes. Alain liked the countryside and loved going to his grandmother's farm to look after the animals and drive the tractor. Even today, he only really feels at ease in the country. *"I could have been a countryman. In fact, by necessity, I spend most of my time in town and while it's true that I love cities like Paris, Rome or London, I never spend more than two or three days at a time in town. If I could chose, I'd live in the country."* Of course, these people had no idea about motor racing as they never dream of things that are totally inaccessible to them because of their social and cultural standing. All in all, the Prost family situation was best described as comfortable. The hard work was paying off and "Toutube" was doing well during this period. André and Marie-Rose decided to offer themselves a little luxury as a reward and they now acquired an apartment on the Côte d'Azur. The family would troop down there once a year for the month of August to enjoy a well-deserved summer break. The kids all loved the holiday fun and it looked as though nothing much could change the well paced life of this family from the Loire when, one very fine day in the summer of 1970, the youngest boy experienced something that would turn his life upside down. *"It's what I must do,"* he promised himself. *"It's amazing!"*

André Prost came from the Jura and he met Marie-Rose Karatchian at the start of the Fifties. They had two boys, Daniel, born in 1953 and Alain, two years later on 24th February 1955. Alain was born in the neighbouring village of Lorette, but lived in St Chamond, thus becoming a "couramiaud" in local parlance. The word has its origins in a ceremony which took place on the eve of Saint Jean day (24th June.) A large bonfire is lit in the Place de l'Observatoire. In the old days, the square was part of the College of Canons who were zealous in their duties. In the middle of the square, a large tree from the nearby forest was planted in a base of coal, also locally produced. A cat was tied with a rope to its base, to symbolise the devil. The poor beast would

fight... like a devil. Sometimes its short life would end in the flames. The locals saw this as a symbol of purification as a result of trial by fire. Sometimes the cat managed to escape the hellish fire, which was seen as a sign that the demons had left their human hosts. The bravest would set off in pursuit of their feline prey, even climbing trees in an effort to catch it. People from the neighbouring areas of Saint-Etienne and Rive de Gier thus referred to the people from Chamond as "court à miaou" or "cat chasers." There was an element of disdain in their tone which characterised all rivalries in the area.

Alain was a good child and rarely in trouble, but he was a ball of energy and he always had an overriding need to expend it somehow. Sport had

never figured on the family's agenda, but in 1963, the Prost family had to change its thinking and the little lad joined the local football club, the Olympic. A few years later, young Alain was taken in hand by the highly rated Centre de Formation de Saint-Etienne and the dream began. For French lovers of the round ball game, the name of the Geoffroy-Guichard stadium meant the powerful "Green" team, who were multiple French champions thanks to star players like Hervé Revelli, Robert Herbin, Jean-Michel Larqué and Aimé Jacquet. Alain Prost is an ardent supporter of his local team, the A.S.S.E. He has no particular favourites, but supports the entire team. For him, the idea of team spirit, to the detriment of the individual is and always will be of great

● **4**_Marie-Rose and André Prost never tried to discourage their young lad from pursuing his ambitions on four wheels and, according to the man himself, "were quite cool about it all."
(DPPI)

importance. It even applied when he was at the height of his powers on four wheels. His father would give in to the incessant nagging and take the lad to see his heroes play. So the men of the Prost clan would pile into the father's car and head off for the "green cauldron of hell" as the famous stadium was known. As he approached adolescence, life for young Alain revolved around school, friends who lived near home, football and work for the family. He was not exactly keen on school and settled for keeping his head down and going unnoticed, doing just enough to move up a grade each year. He liked the company of his friends, but this was limited by the football training and having to work at home. Apart from his favourite sport, Alain had little time for dreaming, certainly not about cars and other such madness, but his brother did it for him. He liked motorised sports, especially motorbikes. Just as Alain got his hands on his first Motobecane moped, Daniel moved up a gear to a Testi with six speeds! As for cars, they were far from their thoughts. The Prost family's social status was a long way off flashy cars and Alain was more likely to show an interest in the Citroen "Tube," the company's delivery van, rather than his father's car. The "Tube" which transported the family's wares was typical of the pragmatic and practical attitude of André and Marie-Rose which allowed them to provide a relatively comfortable life for their children. Everything they owned, they owed to their own efforts, but events of Spring 1968 would even affect the sleepy house at 21 rue Dugas-Montbel.

As the paving stones flew through the night sky around Paris in what has come to be known as the "student's revolt," the smooth running of French industry would begin to grind slowly to a halt. The entire country was about to be caught up in the events taking place in its capital city and André Prost's business was no exception. One morning in May, his workforce opted for industrial action, stopping work. While André could understand their reasons, he could not accept their actions. He felt he had created an atmosphere of mutual trust and a sense of family within his small business and he was sad and hurt by this ingratitude. Stung by their action, he shut up shop, packed his entire family into a Citroen DS and headed south for their apartment in Cannes. Once the mood had passed, he decided to make the most of what the area had to offer at that time of year and that is how he and his two sons found themselves queuing outside a wooden ticket booth in Monaco, buying three cheap seats for the Formula 1 grand prix. André, Daniel and Alain found themselves near the harbour chicane, having to stand on a low wall to watch the cars whiz by. Alain found the

spectacle entertaining, especially when there were accidents and enjoyed his day. But the experience left no more lingering effects than a visit to a funfair or an animal park. Nevertheless, André bought tickets again two years later and this time, Alain appreciated the event for what it was. He remembered the Formula 3 race, won by Jean-Pierre Jaussaud, Johnny Servoz-Gavin's mishap in qualifying for the Formula 1 race and Jochen Rindt's pursuit of Jack Brabham in the race.

No sooner back in Saint-Chamond, the Monegasque weekend was consigned to the ranks of a pleasant memory as Alain was once again 100% immersed in his love for football: *"I got through the trials to be a professional footballer,"* he recalls today. *"It was at Vichy and happened along with entry to a physical education course in Lyon. My aim was to try and earn my living somehow from sport. But I was slightly handicapped by my small size for the position I played – right wing – where you needed to be quite forceful."* Then, one day, as he crossed the ball, he injured his knee and immediately afterwards, just before the 1970 summer holidays, broke his wrist doing an exercise on the beam. Much to his disgust, he faced the prospect of a month in Cannes with his arm in plaster! He could forget about football, swimming and other water sports. The summer break which he had been looking forward to so eagerly now spread out as a boring time with nothing to do, something the young man could not cope with.

At La Siesta, near Antibes, there was an amusement park that also boasted a small karting track. For just a few francs, you could have a go at the wheel of an old wheezy fourstroke kart. Daniel Prost was looking out for his little brother, who was beginning to find time dragging and began pestering his parents to take them to the track. Mum and Dad finally capitulated and Alain tucked his broken arm under a jumper. The minimum age requirement was sixteen, so Marie-Rose had to sign a waver for the people who ran the track, so that her youngest son could drive. He got in the seat, hardly a race cockpit and could only steer one-handed. The fun turned into a mini-competition and before long, Alain Prost was passing everyone else. At the end of the allotted fifteen minutes, the young lad extricated himself from the kart. He was shaken and his head was spinning. When one sits in a kart for the very first time, the meagre 40 km/h it struggles to achieve seems like double that, maybe even more. That, along with the need to make rapid decisions and take action, planning how to overtake had provoked new and powerful sensations. Then, after having another go a few days later, Alain saw the light: *"This is what I have to do. It's amazing!"*

"Are you mad?" was André and Marie-Rose's reaction when Alain informed them he intended having a crack at karting. No sooner was he back from his holidays than he got in touch with the local clubs and without wasting a moment, he put his name down to join the one at Rive de Gier. He had none of the equipment needed to take part, nor did he have the 700 francs which one of his friends wanted for his Mercadier-McCulloch. He then embarked on a plan which speaks volumes about his determination and tenacity which would later mark him out as a future champion. He decided to save money wherever he could to rustle up a nest egg so that he could buy a kart and he did it all in secret! When his parents gave him money to go to the cinema with his friends, he would pocket it and then not see the film. He offered to go and do the shopping, hanging on to the few centimes of change and would horde every last franc his father gave him for helping out in the workshop. For Christmas, he warned everyone: "I don't want presents, just cash." He did not go out and concentrated all his energies on the target he had fixed himself. Everyone noted the lad's strange behaviour, but no one ever found out what he was up to. Then, one day, Alain announced that he was finally going to buy the Mercadier-McCulloch, laying out his patiently acquired savings that had taken a year to amass. There was much strained laughter in the Prost household, but faced with their son's determination, Marie-Rose and André capitulated, believing it was only a passing fad.

As far as Alain was concerned it was far more than that. He had made his decision and his life was now organised around this new passion. That is the way he is in that as soon as he discovers something new, he wants to see it through to the end. He studied the subject, reading magazines and taking an interest in the technical side. Years later, the same applied when he took up golf and cycling. He knew nothing about motor sport, so he set out to learn at first hand what it was all about, jumping on his moped, on his own most of the time, heading off to watch a rally or other event. "I was a bit crazy," he admits with a smile. "I remember once going to the Rallye du Forez on my Mobylette, when it was raining cats and dogs. I had found a sort of mini cave where I spent the whole night waiting for the cars to come by in the early morning. I was mainly interested in the technical side, so I would go and look at the cars close up. Then, indirectly, I got interested in the drivers. I especially remember the epic battles between Maublanc and Mieusset in the hillclimbs, Darniche and his NSU in the Rallye du Forez. But, and it's still the case today, I cannot separate the human element from the technical side." One day, he even went as far as to pack his rucksack and set off for the legendary Nurburgring for a motorcycle rally. His trek ended at Lyon… because of snow! The young boy was completely unaware of the worry he caused his parents. He would announce that he was setting off on another trip and they had to deal with it. It was yet another example of Alain Prost's character coming to the fore: when he has decided on something, nothing can make him deviate from it and he will stay with it to the bitter end.

From then on, things moved fast. He bought that famous kart and soon realised it involved more time working on it than driving. But the need to dismantle everything all the time laid the groundwork for an excellent technical baggage. It was now 1971 and Alain Prost was about to take the decision which would shape his destiny outside those arenas with a green pitch in the middle. The grey asphalt would now be his daily home and everything would follow on from that. He gave up soccer for good in 1972 as, in any case, his injured knee ruled out any chances of making it at a national level. He gave up school first and then the Physical Education course, finally asking his father to take him on in the family business which was short of manpower at the time. When Alain had proudly shown him his 700 francs, his father had said, "you fiddled about to get them, well now you can fiddle about for the rest." However, he realised his son was at the point of no return and in a conciliatory move, offered him a proper job. He even let him use a corner of the workshop to fettle his kart. Alain had just turned seventeen, about to embark on a career that would last twenty one years in motor sport at the highest level. It was a career launched thanks to a few laps at the wheel of a mediocre rental kart, driven with his arm in plaster! ∎

• **6**_Soon, the little "cat chaser" would be transformed into a redoubtable trophy chaser; trophies which he stockpiled in his father's house.
(DPPI)

Chapter 3
1973–1975
First successes, first crashes

(voir parge 13)

Alain PROST

Lyonnais

encore vainqueur

• **8**_The first press cuttings. One can see the adverb "encore" (yet again) underlining the fact that young Prost from Lyon was at it again, wearing his first green and white check helmet. He drove a Taifun kart with a very upright position for the steering wheel, which he was very keen on.
(Joseph Dimier Archive)

Alain soon made his mark on the local karting tracks. With his obsolete material he managed to match the more experienced and better equipped drivers. He was kind to his equipment, while still being aggressive on the track and his driving style was already blessed with finesse which worked wonders. His first supporters were his parents, who soon cast aside their initial reticence. *"My mother was always very scared for me and was there to add psychological support. She never watched the race. She would go for walks in the countryside. One day, in Holland, she went so far she got lost and someone had to bring her back."* His father decided to attend the races, if only to provide transport and lend a hand. For his first official race at Hauteville, he had to borrow a chassis off a friend as his did not conform to the regulations. His performance however was another matter! Another problem for the diminutive and slender Alain was that, by changing class, he had to take on an additional twenty kilos of ballast to meet the minimum weight requirement. During a collision, he rolled the kart and some lead weights which he had stuck in his pockets – karting enthusiasts will be amused to learn – fell out onto the track, much to the annoyance of the officials. However, they showed leniency towards the little beginner, who thanked them by finally winning the race. All in all, this first year was a learning season and Alain stayed in the local area. The League races run on temporary tracks served to help him get to grips with the sport and develop a better understanding of this new world and of the mechanical side of the sport. The chief lesson Alain learned was that his dear Mercadier-McCulloch, his first object of desire, was no longer really up to the mark. Along with his father, he was determined to set up a serious race programme for 1973, so young Prost sold his first kart to buy something with which he could battle it out at the front of the pack. He acquired a Vacquand chassis, which would be traded in during the season for a Taifun, powered by a 100 cc Parilla, one of Italy's benchmark engines.

In karting, it is not enough to have the latest engine. The difference comes from the quality of preparation thus allowing the driver to chase after those final hundredths or even thousandths needed for a top performance. The Rive de Gier club had a locally rated tuner, Jean-Pierre Gauthier. He lived in Chesnay dans les Yvelines, not far from the famous Thiveral track where Alain would experience mixed fortunes. The Prost family duly went knocking on Gautier's door so that he could look after the Parilla SS20 engines that the champion in the making would use that season. After the usual Rhone-Alpes League events, Alain's first major foray outside his home area took him to Sochaux where he secured the 1973 French Junior championship. Although he was pleased with this first title, Alain Prost was not exactly ecstatic about it. He appreciated its worth as a reward for a job well done. He simply tried to apply himself to this newly-discovered discipline which he enjoyed. That was all. A trip to Holland would alter his perception.

As they first set foot in the paddock at Oldenzaal for the Europe Juniors championship, the Prost family were awestruck. *"They already had trucks and trailers and we arrived with a trailer which I knocked together with the help of a handyman friend of my parents! I was not big headed and did not expect to be dominant. I had confidence, but I was already apprehensive about the next day and the next race. I won nearly all the heats and then the final. In fact, it was a surprise to me. It was from that race that realisation dawned. I told myself I might have a future ahead of me."* Boosted by these two consecutive championship wins, the young Prost decided to try for the triple and, one week later, he entered the French International championship at the Thiverval circuit, in the Yvelines department close to Paris. The track is tucked in tight to the folds of a little verdant and quiet valley just outside the little town of Plaisir and its layout is varied and demanding. Alain stamped his authority on it, finishing second behind a young and experienced Parisian, Jean-Louis Bousquet. He used a BM engine, also prepared by Jean-Pierre Gauthier. One man kept a close watch on this young phenomenon. He was the track owner and ran a shop, la Sovame, in the Paris suburb of Aubervilliers and he also ran the French team. He was a major player in the little world of French karting and well respected. Naturally, Michel Fabre cornered the young man to find out more.

A few weeks later, Alain Prost bumped into Michel Fabre again in the pits at Nivelles-Baulers in Belgium for the world championship.

Accompanied as ever by his father, the young lad had decided to come and try his luck up against the kings of the category, truth be told with little hope of getting much of a result. Eventually, he finished 14th, an honourable performance in such a big event, which was won by Ireland's Terry Fullerton. Obviously, Alain did not have the same level of equipment and had no support, apart from the valuable assistance of his tuner, Jean-Pierre Gauthier, whose role went no further than the end of the exhaust pipes on the Parilla. André therefore asked Michel Fabre to look after his son over the coming years in the hopes of building an international career.

Fabre summoned Prost for a series of tests at the Thiverval circuit. At the time, Sovame built its own chassis with the help of one of the most sought after tuners at the time, Italy's Franco Baronni, who would help fellow countrymen like Riccardo Patrese and Elio de Angelis to name but two, to victory. The test sessions were indeed productive. Fabre was bowled over by the volume of work and the technical feeling of the driver, while Prost discovered the delights of fine tuning when it came to tyres and chassis. An agreement was quickly reached: Sovame would take Prost on board as from the start of 1974, supplying him will all equipment (the Parilla engines replaced with Komet ones) as well as all the back-up needed to challenge for international honours. It was no small deal. Sovame were the French distributors of all parts from the famous Italian company, IMAE, which built the best engines and parts, essential to compete at the highest level.

● **9**_The little French gang at the European junior championships at Oldenzaal in the Netherlands: (from left to right) Terreaux, Perrin, Prost, Ferté and Jallageas. *(Joseph Dimier Archive)*

Michel Fabre: "A jumper worth 8 tenths"

In some ways, Michel Fabre was Alain Prost's first team manager, if one can apply this term to an age and a discipline which was still a long way off the rarified and elitist world of the top levels of motor sport. He recalls the exceptional finesse and sensitivity of his young charge.

"His greatest quality was the ability to explain what the kart was doing, how the chassis and engine were reacting at certain points. 90% of drivers would tell you, 'the kart isn't holding the road, I can't steer or brake' and that would be it. Alain could describe in detail what was going on and that was a great help to the people working with him. But he had no technical training, just very accurate judgement. That's where he made the difference. He looked at every detail and was extremely punctilious and demanding. He was a "pain in the arse" in the good sense of the phrase. He could spend up to an hour working on the position of the seat in a new chassis, which is an important detail! One incident will always stick in my mind. At the '74 world championships in Estoril, he was not on the pace in first practice. Jannick Auxemery and I were out on track and we called him in. By the time we got back to the pits, he'd gone out again, so we went back to watch and suddenly, 8 tenths quicker! He was now doing similar times to the best, like Goldstein, Patrese, Cheever and de Angelis. Once we were all back in the pits, he said to us: "You'll never believe this, but my jumper was bothering me, so I took it off."

Official support from the Mecca of karting was a guarantee of being able to fight with the best on level terms. Although, as we will see, a couple of tiny differences can nevertheless create significant gaps.

Back in his native Loire, Alain Prost was to face the first dilemma of his career. Naturally enough, Michel Fabre was not the only one to have been impressed by the performance of the champion apprentice and the Italian BM factory, one of the top companies in its field, made him a stupendous offer: works driver status for 1974, with all the advantages that go with the supply of the very best equipment on offer and a monthly salary of 2000 francs! One has to realise that at this point in Alain's career, it was an incredible offer, both in terms of a step up the professional ladder and financially. But it was an offer which came with a host of questions as to how it would work out. On top of that, Prost had given Michel Fabre his word. His ambition told him to say yes to the Italians, but his honesty commanded him to turn it down politely. Honesty won the day.

In 1974, firmly handled by Jannick Auxemery, Alain Prost made the step from gifted amateur to confirmed professional. Auxemery was a former driver who earned his spurs in Formula Renault at the start of the Seventies. Having decided to give up racing to devote himself to karting, he was an effective second in command to Michel Fabre and was pretty much the sporting director at Sovame. He took the young Prost in hand and inculcated him with the good habits that would stay with the driver throughout his career. The result was a year peppered with strokes of brilliance, with the French senior championship title as its crowning glory. On the financial front, Alain was to become fully self-sufficient this year. Unlike BM, Fabre could not pay him but came up with another deal: Sovame did not have a dealer in the Rhone-Alpes region and he handed Prost the chance to take on the role and see what he could make of it. Thus did Prost the driver become Prost the businessman by importing the Italian kit into his area. The word "businessman" should be seen as something of an honorary title, given that Prost did not have much time to devote to the venture. *"He was sort of our representative,"* recalls Michel Fabre, *"but he did not do it for very long. His father was actually more involved because Alain wasn't there very much. In fact, he had just taken it on to cover some of his expenses given that we supplied all his equipment."* The young man also turned himself into a tuner for some of his most faithful customers, thus picking up enough money to see him through to the end of every month.

• **12**_ At the Creusot track in 1974, Alain Prost becomes French senior champion. This much wanted title would open the doors to the world of car racing. *(DPPI)*

When he showed up at the Creusot track in the Loire region for the French senior championships, Alain was now considered one of the favourites, having been so dominant that season. The pundits were proved right as Prost was majestic from start to finish. His speed and above all, his great consistency saw him take the win in the finals. The French title came with a bursary for the winner to tackle a course at a racing school. It was one of Alain's clear objectives when he entered this race and he decided to wait until 1975 to take up this very welcome prize. For the time being, he preferred to concentrate on what would be another important step.

That year, the world championships were held at the Estoril track in Portugal. Alain was back on the international trail, meeting up with Italian stars like Riccardo Patrese and the American, Eddie Cheever. More importantly, he would be going up against Belgium's François Goldstein who pulled off the tour de force of winning the world title four times in 1969, '70, 71' and '72! All these guys were battle hardened warriors, who were not beyond the odd devious deed to come out on top and Alain would soon learn that lesson. In the meantime, battle raged as expected, but poor Prost never even got to take part: a bit light on the engine front, which showed the importance of having "works" status

as mentioned earlier and also light on experience. He made do with watching the Italian-Belgian confrontation which went in Patrese's favour.

At the end of 1974, Alain decided to bring forward his call-up to military service *"to get this pain out of the way as soon as possible."* He was stationed in Treves in Germany. He was given a cushy job as a secretary and one of his thrilling jobs was filling in leave forms and he tackled it with particular zeal, especially when it came to his own! 1975 was going to be a key year and he was not prepared to miss out on any of the major meetings through having to "serve his country." The first of these meetings was the traditional Alazar challenge, organised that year by Michel Fabre at Thiverval. This early season race would decide the make up of the French team for forthcoming international events and so it was imperative to put on a good show. The essential ingredients in terms of drivers were basically French, peppered with a few big name foreigners, including François Goldstein. He won, closely followed by Alain Prost, who did not even wait for the end of the victory lap to punch him in the face! A fistfight then broke out between the mechanics from both camps and the furious Alain saw his license suspended by the Federation for six months. In his defence, Alain was convinced, and still is today, that he had been deliberately knocked off the track by one of the Belgian champion's team-mates on the last lap. Then, having got back on track without losing the lead, he was hit from behind by Goldstein himself in the final corner. According to Michel Fabre, Goldstein did not hit him from behind, but leaned on him "forcefully" on the inside of the turn, thus punting the Frenchman off the track. What really enraged Prost was that, no sooner had they crossed the line, than François offered him a handshake. *"If the only reason for him nudging me was that he was trying to get past, I could have accepted it,"* confides Alain. *"But that he offered me his hand in this sly way, I could not bear it."* It was a hard blow for the pig headed young man, convinced he was the victim of a carefully contrived plot, while Goldstein always denied it in public. Fabre then intervened with the Federation, arguing that it could not rob itself of its best driver over such a slight misdemeanour. Begrudgingly, the officials had to admit the sense of the argument and lifted the ban. Another "injustice" would come the young man's way a few months later in the French championship.

At the Rochefoucault track in Charente, Alain was up against two main opponents: his own team-mate, Patrick Terreau, with whom he took a joint pole position and Marc Boulineau, an experienced driver who came late to karting. Prost soon sorted them both out, building up a comfortable lead in the final. But he slightly lost concentration after a badly handled period when the race was neutralised following an accident where a driver had been injured and Alain was passed by Boulineau with two laps to go. Having woken himself up, Alain charged up behind Marc, catching him almost within sight of the flag. In the final corner, he slotted down the inside, pushing his rival into the run off area. Prost took the chequered flag as the winner and was French champion for the second year in a row! A few minutes later, it was fisticuffs again between the mechanics from the two teams – yes, again! And the Boulineau clan protested, claiming Prost's move had been dangerous. After a quick meeting of the officials, who called it on their own, they decided to disqualify the winner!

Prost was gobsmacked and wanted to know more. No one dared say anything to him and Michel Fabre has his own ideas on the subject. *"Boulineau raced for Birel. The Birel importer and his mates from La Rochefoucault were so desperate to win that they made one hell of a fuss. I went to see Mr. Alazar and said to him, "you can't just disqualify the guy like that. It has to be heard by a sporting commission. "Alain was distraught: it was a racing incident, just like the one with Goldstein. He still talks to me about it and as I said to him once, "what on earth are you bothered about? You've been Formula 1 world champion four times. He replied, "you cannot imagine how much it bothers me."* Just like his future alter-ego in Formula 1, Ayrton Senna, Alain will never forgive certain slights even with such an illustrious racing career to his name. Just like a musician who laments the one little wrong note at the end of the concert that was regarded as perfect by its audience, they can never accept those small dark moments that, to them, blight their blindingly bright careers. How can we mere spectators understand?

The passion for karting still burnt deeply within Alain, but events were now to turn him away from his first love. The 1975 world championship with its controversial circuit, artificially marked out with straw bales within the Paul Ricard circuit certainly did nothing to help. François Goldstein took his fifth and final world title. Prost gave it his all, but a crash with Terry Fullerton put an end to his slim chances. However, by now he already his heart and mind set on the neighbouring car racing track where, for some time now, he had been getting to grips with a racing car.

Time is a great healer and has now brushed aside the rancour, leaving the more pleasant memories. These days, Prost is happy to recall the highlights of his time behind the wheel of a kart and maintains that, apart from a Formula 1 car, a kart is the most exciting thing to drive. In 1976, he took part in the 24 Hours of Brignoles in the Var region and after that came a long wait until 1993 when he found himself again at the controls of one of these lively machines. He won the first Elf Masters at Paris-Bercy. While that event was no more than a high class demonstration, he took part in the more serious 200 km of Angerville endurance race in the Essonne at the invitation of Michel Fabre. He was teamed up with Gilles, Michel's son. Twenty years on, he found himself up against his old rival, Marc Boulineau, who never left the world of karting. At the time of writing, Marc runs one of the top national endurance racing teams. These days, despite a busy schedule, the four times Formula 1 world champion has acquired for himself and son Nicolas a kart built by a former Italian F1 driver and sometimes turns up at a track in the Jura just to enjoy the pleasure of driving, as do thousands of unknowns every Sunday. ∎

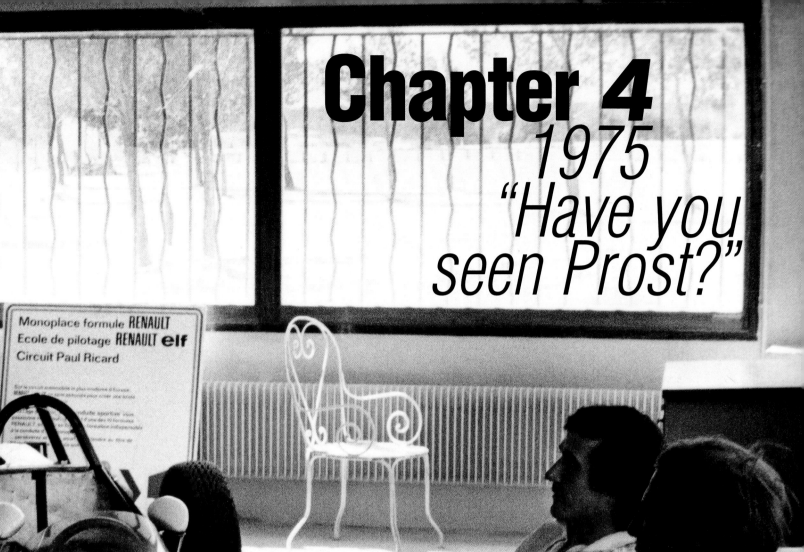

Chapter 4
1975
"Have you seen Prost?"

● **14**_In 1975, Prost the pupil first tackled the 2,200 metres of the little school circuit nestling at the back of the Paul Ricard Grand Prix track. To take part in the Saturday sessions, the young soldier left his garrison in Treves in Germany on a Friday night, arriving at Lyon-Perrache at one in the morning, to be met by his mother. He would sleep a few hours, borrow his mother's car and drive non-stop to get to the circuit in the south of France on Saturday morning.
Then, sometimes he would also race a kart at Thiverval on the Sunday!
(DPPI)

When he made his karting debut in 1972, Alain Prost could see no further than the end of his accelerator and brake pedals on his little machine. Things changed during the course of '75. His performances had seen him grow in confidence in his future, a future that would not tarry long on the kart tracks. The logical progression for an apprentice racer was to move to cars and the best way to do that was to sign up for one of the famous "Volants," racing school programmes which had become a breeding ground for champions. Prost read about the likes of Cevert, Laffite, Arnoux, Pironi and Tambay, to mention the best known, in the specialist press. He chose to sign up with the Winfield School at the Paul Ricard circuit for what he regarded as three key reasons: the circuit

hosted the Formula 1 French Grand Prix (it might always come in useful later,) it was close to the family apartment in Cannes, which would be handy for somewhere to stay and finally, the weather was always good. Nevertheless, it turned out to be a rainy day when he first showed the world what he could do.

Antoine Raffaelli, a jovial chap from Marseille and Simon de Lautour, a Francophile Englishman ran the school. They were in the habit of watching the progress of their young charges from one end of the short 2.2 km track, at the back of the international circuit. The only thing that struck them about Prost was that his braking technique was far from by the book, braking late under load on the way into a corner (see Antoine Raffaelli's eyewitness account.) On

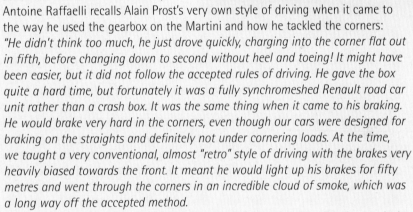

Antoine Raffaelli: "An unconventional driving style"

As co-director of the Winfield school at the Paul Ricard circuit, Antoine Raffaelli recalls Alain Prost's very own style of driving when it came to the way he used the gearbox on the Martini and how he tackled the corners: *"He didn't think too much, he just drove quickly, charging into the corner flat out in fifth, before changing down to second without heel and toeing! It might have been easier, but it did not follow the accepted rules of driving. He gave the box quite a hard time, but fortunately it was a fully synchromeshed Renault road car unit rather than a crash box. It was the same thing when it came to his braking. He would brake very hard in the corners, even though our cars were designed for braking on the straights and definitely not under cornering loads. At the time, we taught a very conventional, almost "retro" style of driving with the brakes very heavily biased towards the front. It meant he would light up his brakes for fifty metres and went through the corners in an incredible cloud of smoke, which was a long way off the accepted method.*
He could judge perfectly when to accelerate again and just how hard to push the throttle without losing drive. He was as consistent as a metronome. And more than that, he knew just how to manage it, depending on how much grip he was getting from the wheels. Once, when he was in F1, I asked to sit alongside him for a few laps of the track, to see how he did it. And I realised that he did not necessarily take the ideal line when the grip levels meant he could take a tighter and therefore shorter line. That was the gist of his secret. In the double right at the Beausset (Paul Ricard) for example, which was a real test, he took a much shorter line than most of the other F1 drivers."

top of that, he did not use the sacrosanct heel and toe method, quite simply because coming from karting, he did not know how to do it and so he crashed through the box on the down-changes. They tried to teach him this technique on the school's old Renault Estafette, but Alain decided to change nothing about his driving style. One should not read into this that some rebellious spirit was at work here. It was just an example of his typically solid pragmatic approach: why bother changing anything when he was quicker than anyone driving in the way he felt most comfortable? Rafaelli finally came round to favouring this style of driving, which he regarded as a more modern approach, but de Latour remained inflexible when it came to the basics. He could just about get by without heel

and toeing, but he insisted that his pupil at least brake in a straight line! The wily Prost then found a solution: in the three corners under Antoine's surveillance, he braked through the corner, while in front of Simon, he made a great show of braking down the straight! Despite his acknowledged speed, Prost did not immediately stand out from all the other pupils at the school. Then one day, going against Alain's predictions as to the weather, the clouds gathered and a persistent rain soaked the track. Kicking up impressive plumes of spray, the little Martini-Renault cars kept filing past the two instructors and the truth was revealed. *"Simon and I split the circuit between us,"* recalls Antoine Raffaelli *and that day, we noticed someone doing some fantastic things, showing a great mastery of* sliding the car with an exceptional sense of balance compared to the others. At the end of the run, Simon came over to me and we both spoke at the same time: "did you see Prost?" We were astounded, because we were already running the cars at high revs and he had put on a really stunning demonstration." The general view that the Frenchman was never comfortable in the rain is certainly worth re-examining, but we will return to that subject in greater detail when we get to an incident in 1982 that would completely change his view of the subject.

When one tries to unravel the factors that separate an excellent driver from a major champion, one invariably comes to the fact that the champion will always have chosen the right car at the right time. Alain Prost's attitude in the semi-finals of the 1975 Elf scholarship already illustrates the character of the man we are dealing with. The two semi-finals were scheduled over two days and the running order was decided at random. Alain was to race on the first day. Out of character, he arrived very late for the briefing, his head down and mumbling feeble excuses. Antoine Raffaelli recalls the scene with some amusement. "We gave him a ticking off! Simon always said 'the most important attribute for a driver is precision!' and he was in a rare old mood. 'I don't care if it's Prost, he won't race!' I replied that he could not forbid our best hope from taking part in the final. In the end, he gave in, but knocked Prost back to the following day's race. And that was exactly what Alain had wanted. He had pulled the wool over our eyes and his lateness was just a ruse! It meant he could stand alongside me throughout the Saturday session to see how the cars behaved, to see which one locked up its wheels the most often and which one set the best lap times the most often. He basically saw the whole picture." This plan says a lot about the cool and calculating attitude of the future champion and the result of it was that Prost was able to chose the best car and easily qualify for the final, due to take place a fortnight later.

The big day arrived on 25th October 1975. Prost had managed to get out of his military obligations, thanks to a false pass-out that he had given himself, having used up his allowed quota with his constant to and fro trips from the barracks to the circuits. The stakes were high: if he failed, he knew that his dream of racing glory would come to an end. But he never even considered the possibility of failure. *"How can one think of failing in the final? It's impossible. I was there to win!"* In order to be sure of total concentration, he insisted that those close to him, Michel Fabre, Jannick Auxemery and his family did not attend. There was an impressive panoply of stars from the racing firmament at the track that day, including Ken Tyrrell, which was enough to put the wind up the toughest competitor. Alain was in determined mood as he stepped into his blue Martini. Before completing the five decisive laps that would decide the outcome of the Volant, he reeled off his three warm-up laps at a pace that already impressed the jury, given that he beat the lap record! Then he did three breathtaking laps, before slowing for the final two, to avoid the risk of any mishap. He was the only driver to get under the five minute barrier and there were no doubts in his mind. The jury's deliberation was swift and clear and Alain Prost won the 1975 Volant Elf and the bursary that went with it. With the pressure finally lifted, he rushed for the phone to announce the good news to his parents, his fiancée Anne-Marie, as well as his faithful friends, Fabre and Auxemery. ■

Chapter 5
1976-1977
Heading for Renault

The chrysalis had become a butterfly. After the sheltered environment of the karting world, it was now time for cars and independence. In 1976, Alain Prost was to embark on a season of Formula Renault and put a compact crew together to look after his little Martini Mk 17 with the engine prepared by Bernard Mangé. He took on his own mechanic, Jean-Pierre Nicolas, had the use of a transporter on loan from Elf and he camped out at the back of the Magny-Cours circuit in a caravan. The track bore no relation to the one that was created in the Nineties and there was a rural and rather convivial atmosphere about it. Tico Martini was set up in a workshop nearby and the young Alain soon headed off to talk to him. *"Right from the start, I realised that with between 30 and 40 of us all in the running, it was a case of making the difference in some other way than behind the wheel, because you can never be sure of anything. So we did a lot of testing to get to understand the chassis and tyres and I think we stole a significant march in that area. I have a lot of respect for Tico, who is the sort of guy who has left his mark on motorsport in his country."*

That year, 1976, Alain Prost was going to leave his mark on the history of Formula Renault. He totally dominated, crushed and all but humiliated the opposition. He won the first 12 races out of 13 counting towards the French Championship, took 6 pole positions and 11 fastest race laps! He took the title after just eight races, in July at Magny-Cours. Such superiority naturally sparked suspicion and resentment amongst the opposition. The finger of suspicion was pointed at the tyres, then the fuel and finally the engines. Calm about it all, Alain lent one of his engines to a sceptical rival who could do no better than with his own power plant! Once his achievements were proved to be "legitimate," Prost became the reference point and everyone else settled for being "the best of the rest." Patrice Lavergne raised his arm in triumph when he managed to come second at Albi. At Rouen, Yves Le Strat was one of his most dangerous rivals and he was so surprised to pass the champion under braking, that he lost concentration and went off two corners later. At Albi again, Prost was in the first heat. He was in the habit of tackling the long right hander after

Christian Courtel: "He was already concerned about his image"

Chief editor of the French weekly "Auto Hebdo" from its first issue in 1976, back then, Christian Courtel was covering national races and was thus able to keep up with the young Prost whom he got to know well: *"It was at Magny-Cours, when he took his third consecutive win that I began to be surprised by the chap's attitude. We hardly knew one another and he came to see me saying, "I hope you're going to write a special feature in your magazine because I've just pulled off something special." I looked at him and asked for an explanation. "Yes, I'm the first scholarship winner to win the first three races in a row." Generally, the drivers never asked for anything. If they won they knew it would be written about. But Alain had made a point of coming to see me to ask me to gild the lily somewhat. He was already concerned about getting himself talked about so that he could then go fishing for sponsors. I realised this was a guy who knew where he was heading. He definitely stood out from the pack in terms of his personality and I was particularly struck by one of his comments. It was July and he was going to take the title well before the end of the season. He said to me: "I think my superiority comes from the fact I drive the car, unlike my opponents who tend to let themselves be driven by it. I can't see any other reason." He was always anxious he would be forgotten and so he did everything he could to ensure he was talked about as much as possible. But it was not done in a manipulative way, or at least not in the beginning."*

● **19**_On a start line in 1976, Alain gets his faithful mechanic, Jean-Pierre Nicolas to make an adjustment. It was a habit that stayed with him to the end of his career. *"Out of 199 F1 grands prix, I must have changed something on the grid in at least 150 of them! Between the warm-up at nine o'clock and the race at two, there can be a significant change in temperature."*
(Willy Arnault Archive)

the pits, known as the Virage des Tribunes, flat out, before snicking down a gear and exiting the corner as quickly as he went in. Amazed at this unconventional style of driving, drivers in the second head were tempted to try this method, only for most of them to end up in the grass!

The press and the public were impressed and everyone had a theory as to the unusual driving style of this terror of the tracks. However, he did not give the impression of being quick, as he had a very smooth style, but the stopwatch never lies. Alain was the quickest. Christian Courtel recalls an anecdote that illustrates the point: *"one day I had my eyes opened thanks to Jean-Louis Schlesser. During a practice session, we went from corner to corner on a little scooter to time the drivers through the different sectors. We noticed that strangely, Alain was never the quickest in a sector. There was always a driver who did better, although it was never the same one! Alain was usually second or third quickest. Over a lap, that made the difference. So, he had already picked up his metronomic, calculating style which would be his trademark throughout his career. He always gave the impression he was dragging his heels, but it was an illusion."*

Throughout his first season of car racing, Alain organised his life the same way he went about his racing, methodically and rationally. Unlike most of the other drivers, he had decided to look after his budget himself rather than entrusting it to Elf. Once again, he showed his determination to leave nothing to chance and to keep everything under control. When he travelled to races during the season, he kept a tight rein on the expenses and he rarely spent a night in a hotel. Alain wanted to eat into his budget as little as possible and so the cunning driver would occasionally arrange to get himself "invited" to dinner by people who were on expenses. As a result, he got a reputation for being stingy, which stuck forever and which he is keen to deny to this day. *"I was on a very tight budget. We had to use the cheapest hotels and sometimes we stayed in bed and breakfasts as was the case at Nogaro, or in hostels. And yes, when someone better off than me could pay, I didn't say no. The problem is that later, once you make it to F1, it's the opposite and you end up paying all the time and sometimes it gets crazy! Occasionally, I lent people money and most of the time, I never got it back again. I don't think I'm tight, so if people want to think that, it doesn't really matter too much. On the contrary, I think I have a realistic approach to money, which is the logical result of coming from a humble background and the fact we struggled at first."*

Out on the track, Alain had won over most of his fellow competitors with his warmth and his class. Given his total domination, the bulk of the opposition was resigned to the fact it was beaten and would even have liked to see Prost pull off the unheard of achievement of winning every race. Bolstered by his twelve previous wins, he was in fighting mood therefore when he arrived at the Imola circuit in Italy for the thirteenth and final round of the championship. As usual, he dominated practice, but in qualifying, his ignition started to play up, cutting out unexpectedly. He came into the pits and once on track again, he hurried his Martini round at a crazy rate of knots and qualified in extremis for the final. Prost started from the back of the grid, but he was fired up and charged through the field at an incredible pace and was soon up with the leaders. Unfortunately, the front bodywork cracked after a forceful drive over the kerbs and that affected the cooling of the engine, which overheated and broke. Alain was sick, knowing that it was all down to that ignition problem. But worse still, he then learnt from Bernard Mange that they had found five centimetres of oil floating in the distributor when he had pitted which could have only been because someone had put them there! He was disgusted at the thought that this sabotage had ruined his exceptional season for him and twenty six years later, the bitter disappointment at missing out on the grand slam rankles as much as ever!

To his impressive score card has to be added the huge body blow Alain dealt to the competitors in the Formula Renault Europe race, held on 9th May 1976 at Dijon. He had just won as he pleased in the first three races of the national championship at Le Mans, Nogaro and Magny-Cours and Elf gave him the chance to test himself at a higher level by taking part in this event at the wheel of a Lola-Renault. He was up against tough racers like Dany Snobeck, Alain Cudini, Jean-Louis Bousquet and even Didier Pironi. He only lost the race because of mechanical bothers, having literally made the opposition look ridiculous (see the comments of Willy Arnault.) There was no doubt about it, Alain's personality and aura was much stronger after this edifying experience. Eight days later, he did it again at Zolder at the wheel of the same car. He started from the front row, proving that his Dijon form was no fluke, but he reassured the opposition by going off the track!

(Willy Arnault Archive)

Willy Arnault: "His pole position at Dijon turned the paddock on its head"

A Federation scrutineer seconded to the Formula Renault series, Willy Arnault recalls the action packed Formula Renault Europe race at Dijon in 1976 where a certain Alain Prost made his debut:

"With ten minutes left to go in qualifying, he set off on a quick lap and equalled Cudini's pole time. Amazement in the paddock! Then, he changed the setting on his anti-roll bar and set off again just before the end of the session, alone on the track and therefore with no one to slipstream. At a circuit like Dijon, with its long uphill straight, it was almost impossible to do an outstanding time without getting a tow from another car. The chequered flag was waved at the end of his one lap and the commentator announced, while cannily dragging out the suspense, that the pole time had just been beaten by a full second by...Alain Prost!

After the session, I went to take the results round the motorhomes and I came across Prost talking to Pironi and the championship organisers. They were explaining to Alain that he was there by invitation, but that under no circumstances was he to interfere with the outcome of the championship in which Didier was in the fight for first place. Prost then turned to Pironi and said: "if I am in the lead tomorrow, I will of course let you pass at the end of the race." Pironi, who was on the verge of tears replied, "if you do that you'll screw up my career." So Alain added, "don't worry, I'll do it discretely."

All the drivers got a real mouthful from their team bosses as they had been beaten by a young lad who had never seen the circuit before and was at the wheel of a poorly set up car! Everyone was stunned and so suspicions were raised about the engine, as usual in these situations. I was asked to open it up to check it. I said I was against opening up an engine before a race, for the obvious mechanical reliability reasons. But faced with a wave of resentment, I asked Bernard Mangé just to take the rocker box off so I could check the valve lift. It's a straightforward operation with little risk and does not require any readjustment whatsoever. There was a slight problem when it came to putting it back, when a cork gasket moved slightly, by about a millimetre. But it was enough for poor Alain to gradually lose all his oil during the race and his engine seized five laps from the flag. Pironi won the race, much to the relief of the whole paddock!"

Having passed his first year exam as a car racer with flying colours, Alain Prost, with even more support from Elf, regrouped his little team for an attack on the European championship in 1977. While Formula Renault was fairly straightforward for a young driver coming from karts, Formula Renault Europe provided the nursery slope of learning how to set up a racing car. The young lad would have to demonstrate his skills as a tuner to go up against the tough opposition he had made contact with during those two races in 1976. Bousquet, Snobek, Dallest and Coulon had no intention of handing out anything on a plate and were not in awe of the new star. Prost would really have to fight and had to share the winner's laurels that year, which made his final triumph even more merited.

The most striking aspect of the 1977 season was Alain's extreme consistency. He won six races which outclassed his rivals, but in races where he had no chance of winning, he made sure he picked up enough points to make the difference in the championship. Two second, third and fifth places were enough to grab the crown with a mere three points advantage over Jean-Louis Bousquet (157 to 154!) It goes some way to explain why he was so angry when the clumsy

actions of a backmarker robbed him of a win at Pau. Prost and Bousquet (in that order) had a merciless dogfight through the twisty streets of the town. At the wheel of his Lola, Jean-Louis put Alain under immense pressure and at first, the leader still managed to control the situation. But not for long. With three laps to go, the two men rushed up behind Gianbruno Del Fante, who panicked and moved across the track at the last moment. Prost went into a spin and Bousquet missed the incident by a whisker. Miraculously, Alain found himself facing the right way, but he crossed the line behind Jean-Louis who took his first win of the year.

On the podium, Prost was sulking and Marc Cernaux, representing BP, pompously berated him for being a bad loser. It is a trait which he was accused of at various times during his career and he has an explanation for this reputation: *"Jean-Louis, who I think is a really good driver had the advantage of being a lawyer, or at least he was coming to the end of his studies to become one. He was relatively comfortable financially, whereas I was playing double or quits. François Guiter (Elf) would tell me, "win your championship and you will be back next year. If you don't win then don't take it for granted."* It

• 24_In 1977, Formula Renault Europe became a real racing school for Alain Prost. *"There was total freedom when it came to developing the chassis and aerodynamics. We could work on the wheelbase and sometimes the track and we* had portable scales to work on weight distribution as well as different front bodywork to suit the various track characteristics. Formula Renault Europe was the best formula, maybe even better than Formula 3." (DPPI)

was a case of survival, pure and simple. When people say, "he is a bad loser" they don't understand what that implies. All drivers like me feel it and I agree entirely with Ayrton on this point. We are winners and cannot bear to lose in that way. When I finish second or third and there was nothing I could do about it, you will never see me sulking." Looking at the points difference between Bousquet and Prost at the end of the year, one can actually see what he is on about. But the general public found it hard to swallow and Alain would often have to explain his attitude. On the other hand, Prost proved to be a gentleman eight days earlier in Monaco, when he warmly congratulated Dany Snobeck who had been untouchable on the famous track. On that day, Alain could do nothing about it and had to settle for second. And there were no grumpy expressions.

The incident at Pau brings us back to another Prost character trait. He agonised over everything and lacked self-confidence despite his exceptional results. The ravaged state of his fingernails bears evident testimony to this! Dany Snobeck has an opinion on the matter: *"like all worriers who want to reassure themselves, he left nothing to chance. Maybe that's why he did not find it easy to confide in people. Despite the fact we were good friends, he always had a cautious side. But I had some good times with him and we had some down to earth conversations."* Like all people who are on the way up, he knew how to turn his faults into virtues. This doubt and worry always pushed him to examine his problems in minute detail and he always tried to fully understand every aspect of racing to have the edge so that he could be as sure as possible of beating his opponents. In this respect, he shared his analytic approach with another great champion whom he always admired, Jackie Stewart. ∎

• 25_In the streets of Pau on 22ⁿᵈ May 1977, Alain Prost led the race up to a few laps from the flag. He finished second and could barely contain his anger. (DPPI)

Chapter 6
1978-1979
Staying down and looking good

A mathematics teacher by trade with a passion for racing, Hugues de Chaunac ran a flourishing team that combined Formula 3 and Formula 2 under the name of Oreca. Most of his team consisted of single-seaters from the Tico Martini workshops where Hugues pulled the strings. At the start of 1978, de Chaunac was facing a diabolical timetable as, apart from the two categories mentioned above, he was preparing to run the new Formula 1 team set up by Tico, with René Arnoux as its driver. The man was a workaholic and the increased workload did not frighten him. He also found time to attend some Formula Renault races, looking for "the new hot property." Naturally, this led to meetings with Alain Prost.

The newly-crowned European champion meanwhile had a clear plan mapped out in his head. He wanted to stay under Elf's wing at all costs, as he knew it would lead to Formula 1 via Tyrrell who took on all the French drivers that François Guiter sent his way, or with Renault

which had made its debut at Silverstone the previous year with its funny yellow car and its turbo engine. With this in mind, Alain would have liked to race Formula 2 this year as the final step to Formula 1. He was all the more keen on the idea, having tested himself in this discipline at the wheel of a Kausen-Renault. The two events, wisely run at Nogaro and Estoril gave him a feel for the power of the car, despite a very average chassis and also an idea of the physical demands it made on the driver. But Guiter made it clear there was no seat for him in F2 and that a Formula 3 season would be just as beneficial. With no choice, Prost signed to drive Formula 3 with Oreca in 1978. He would only ever drive a Formula 2 on one more occasion, when he raced a Chevron-Hart at Pau, although his race ended prematurely with a broken clutch.

Renault also made its Formula 3 debut that year with a new four cylinder unit, based on the block of a Renault 20TS. Alain therefore knew what to expect. There was everything to do and the confrontation with the Toyota engine used by the rival teams looked like being a stern test. And so it was. Despite having a good chassis, the Martini Mk21B struggled to keep up with the opposition, especially the Ralt driven by a Brazilian called Nelson Piquet who was blowing the British championship wide open. Piquet made the trip to the continent a few times and thus crossed swords with Prost. Alain likes winners and he could not help himself from feeling drawn to this chap with the piercing look, a haughty manner and a caustic sense of humour. The first time they met at the Castellet, the Frenchman struggled to understand the Brazilian's humour. *"He spoke English badly and I could hardly manage it either. Maybe that's how we hooked up as there was no need to talk."* During the year, Nelson left for the world of Formula 1 and it was only two years later that the two men met up again and forged a lasting friendship. The '78 season was a tough one. The Renault engine lacked power and was unreliable. For the first time since his meteoric rise through the ranks, Alain Prost had to learn how to deal with defeat and how to be patient. By the mid-season, he only had one meagre fourth place at Monaco to show for himself after five races. Alain finally stepped up to the third rung on the podium at Paul Ricard after an entertaining scrap with Piquet. He tried to put his problems to one side and look on the bright side: he was

working with a first rate team at Oreca and he appreciated Hugues de Chaunac's rigorous and rational approach. He got on fine with Robert Descombes, his chief mechanic and he was learning a great deal from technical discussions with the designer of the Renault engine. This engineer was none other than Bernard Dudot, the father of the V6 turbo, which would go on to win that year's Le Mans 24 Hours and, in its 1.5 litre form, powers the company's new Formula 1 car. For the moment, the two men were just at the first stage of a common career path which would cross several times in the future. Over the course of the season, the engine made enormous progress which finally allowed Alain to take a win in the penultimate race, at Jarama. Despite a poor overall result in the European series where he finished ninth, Prost consoled himself by adding to his already impressive track record the title of French Formula 3 champion.

Back in the calm environment of the family home in the rue Dugas-Montbel, the young champion in a hurry looked back at the year just gone and the one coming up. He would turn 24, an ideal age to tackle the final step on the road to Formula 1. At the end of the Seventies, Formula 1 was peppered with Frenchmen heading for the top. The likes of

• **28**_Alain did not have much luck in Formula 2 which he tried his hand at only very rarely. In 1977, a tenth place and a retirement in two races and in 1978, a retirement at the wheel of the Hart-engined Chevron in the streets of Pau.

Laffite, Jabouille, Arnoux and Pironi had all come from Formula 2 and so Alain remained convinced that his initiation would include a stint in this category and that Elf would help him, as it had done for the past three years now.

When François Guiter suggested he "stay down a year" in Formula 3, the ambitious racer fell off his chair. Guiter explained that Elf was no longer too keen on splashing out on the costs of a Formula 2 season, when a well planned Formula 3 campaign would be just as effective. De Chaunac was singing off the same hymn sheet. *"We showed him that dominating in Formula 3 would be just as valuable as taking the risk of only winning a few races in Formula 2, which might or might not happen. All the ingredients were in place. The car was good, the team was well prepared and the engine had made serious progress."* Alain Prost finally agreed to this rational argument and shelved his dreams of grandeur, pumping up his motivation for the 1979 season. If he had to do it again then why not give it his best shot?

As Hugues de Chaunac had predicted, the Martini MK27-Renault package was really competitive that year. Right from the first event at Vallelunga, Prost finished second and set the fastest race lap, then strung together a series of three wins at the Osterreichring, Zolder and Magny-Cours. He finished third at Donington

and finally was able to brandish the trophy from the top step of the most prestigious podium in Monaco, in the race that took place on the Saturday afternoon of the Formula 1 Grand Prix weekend. Winning at Monaco counts for something in a driver's career, be it in F3 or F1, but contrary to popular belief, the Formula 1 team bosses do not instantly drop everything to go in pursuit of the latest rising star. "I imagined that people would watch, but that was not the case," maintained Prost. *"I am not sure if the F1 people watch the Monaco F3 race. Indeed, how many winners at Monaco in F3 have made it into F1?"* As far as de Chaunac was concerned, *"Alain's win did not make any more of an impression than the others. I think it was more to do with the season as a whole, plus Monaco of course, which flicked the switch."*

One month after Monaco, Guy Ligier immediately thought of Prost as a replacement for Patrick Depailler, who had been seriously injured in a hang-gliding accident. There was even a test session, but the matter went no further and in the end, it was Jacky Ickx who drove the JS11. Alain would have another opportunity to get a clear picture of the real state of play when, in August, he turned up in the paddock for the Dutch Grand Prix. He arrived in all his glory, or so he thought. He was practically assured of the European Formula 3

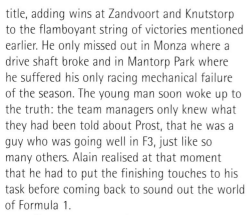

Hugues de Chaunac: "Maximum concentration"

After business studies, Hugues de Chaunac tried his hand as a racing driver at the end of the Sixties, mainly in the Gordini Cup, then in Formula France. He set up the Oreca team in 1972 and it would be a training ground for many aspiring champions such as Patrick Tambay, Didier Pironi and René Arnoux. He recalls Alain Prost's abilities as an organised and calculating driver:

"He has always been very structured. He had a very clear idea of the targets he had set himself and the working methods he wanted to apply to get them. It started with his own approach. His main quality was maximum concentration on the goal he had his sights set on. He learnt then that you had to gather the people around you to do it. Richard Dallest, his team-mate in 1979, was very strong and Alain did not really outclass him. But Alain had a little something extra over Richard in my opinion. He was very methodical and left nothing to chance. Dallest was a brilliant driver but more laid back and relaxed.

I liked Alain's determination and his qualities in terms of setting up the car. As a driver, he never made mistakes, so he never went off the track. Compared with many drivers of his generation who broke the equipment, for us it was a huge advantage. He knew his limits. To do a time he never drove at 120%. He had that rare quality of knowing how to flirt with 100% and so he never went off. When a driver goes off the track it's because he has tried to give 101%."

title, adding wins at Zandvoort and Knutstorp to the flamboyant string of victories mentioned earlier. He only missed out in Monza where a drive shaft broke and in Mantorp Park where he suffered his only racing mechanical failure of the season. The young man soon woke up to the truth: the team managers only knew what they had been told about Prost, that he was a guy who was going well in F3, just like so many others. Alain realised at that moment that he had to put the finishing touches to his task before coming back to sound out the world of Formula 1.

The season ended in a manner worthy of the determination and motivation that the young man possessed. He took three superb wins at Jarama, La Chatre and Albi, added to which he set three fastest race laps and took pole at Jarama. It was a brilliant end to the 1979 season. With nine wins and two podium finishes in 13 races, Alain Prost was crowned European Formula 3 champion in fine style. François Guiter therefore decided it was time to present the little Frenchman to the court of Formula 1. Alain left Europe for the first time in a large Boeing 747 which landed not long after in Canada.

Prost turned up at the Notre-Dame circuit in Montreal to find the paddock dumbstruck by the sudden announcement of Niki Lauda's retirement. Bernie Ecclestone offered Alain the Brabham drive at Watkins Glen in the United States. For his part, Guiter was doing all in his power to secure a drive for his protégé with Ligier. Sadly, neither option came to anything as Ecclestone opted for Ricardo Zunino and Ligier finally went with Didier Pironi. In both cases, it turned out that Alain's pockets were not deep enough. But there was still one ray of hope. Alain was introduced to Patrick McNally who looked after public relations for Marlboro. He came up with the suggestion of a drive for the United States Grand Prix, but Alain remained level headed. *"I told McNally I wanted to do F1 but not in these conditions. I wanted to have a quiet test session first, at Ricard which I knew well, simply because at the time, all the winter testing took place at that track. Everyone thinks I chose Paul Ricard, but that's wrong. I would have gone anywhere except Watkins Glen which I didn't know at all."*

Back home, Alain began to fidget, driving his team mad. He had nothing to do and no one got in touch so the future was uncertain. He had also run out of fingernails! He even seriously considered starting work again in his father's workshop. When Patrick McNally finally rang him to let him that a test had been fixed up for Ricard in November, the entire Prost family could breathe again.

● **31**_ The coronation! Every driver dreams of winning one day in Monaco, be it in Formula 3 or Formula 1. Prost did it on 26ᵗʰ May 1979, on the eve of the Formula 1 Grand Prix.

Prost arrived at the McLaren factory, in Colnbrook to the west of London. Although he was impressed with the reception – a chauffeur at the airport, a fine dinner featuring foie gras, he knew that all this "show" could come to an end at a moment's notice. One mistake or an off-track excursion in the opening laps and the very same chauffeur would be taking him back to the airport. McLaren boss Teddy Mayer was thinking of replacing Patrick Tambay who had not been giving satisfaction and was in any case thinking of switching to the CanAm series. So he took the opportunity on a fine but cold day at the Paul Ricard circuit to try out two potential candidates for the drive: a young American from Formula Atlantic called Kevin Cogan and Alain Prost. Alain climbed into the McLaren M29 and tried to understand the last-minute instructions, as his English was still very basic and set off down the pit lane for the very first time in his life in a car powered by a 470 hp V8! "Your actual thought at this precise moment is that you will not be able to drive the car," recalls Alain. *"It seems huge, whereas in fact it is very small. And bit by bit, as the laps go by, everything closes in. The car gets smaller and smaller, the people get closer and closer and you get the feeling it's beginning to work."* Cogan took over from the Frenchman who had deliberately not spoken to him throughout the test in order to unsettle him and it seemed to work. The American went straight on a couple of times and missed the odd gear change, so Mayer called the session to an end. He had made his choice and Prost got the McLaren contract, while Cogan got the chauffeur to the airport. ∎

• **32**_The winning team of the 1979 season: Alain Prost surrounded by his mechanics with, above him, Robert Descombes, his chief mechanic. Anne-Marie came to join the celebrations with the man she would marry in 1980.

• **33**_One of the most important moments of Alain's career: in November he tries out the Formula 1 McLaren M29 at the Paul Ricard circuit and immediately convinces the entire team, starting with its boss, Teddy Mayer. *(DPPI)*

Chapter 7
1980
A tadpole in a big pond

The team founded by the late Bruce McLaren in 1966 had its glory days in the Seventies with two world titles; one with Emerson Fittipaldi in 1974 and the other with James Hunt in 1976. Since then, it had slowly slipped on a downward spiral of defeat and on the eve of the Eighties, it lived on past glories rather than looking to the future. Nevertheless, for a young driver it still presented a useful way to learn and to try and get noticed. As he became a grand prix driver at the start of 1980, Alain Prost not only discovered competition at the highest level, but the little Frenchman also learnt about the English mentality, which was so different to what he had experienced in France. This small detail would take on a capital importance as we would see later in the development of the future four times world champion's career.

Integration into a British team depends a lot on humour, spiced with a dash of lemon. Prost was immediately nicknamed "Tadpole" because of his size and because he was a little Frog! *"The English like teasing their drivers,"* explains Alain with a smile. *"At the time I was rather taken aback, but it is part of British humour. If you do that in a French team it is not considered the done thing and is not approved of."* On a more serious note, Prost learnt to appreciate British pragmatism, which

he adopted as his own during his thirteen year career in Formula 1. He also appreciated the sound advice from John Watson, his new and experienced team-mate, who was more than willing to help people he liked. *"I don't think I was really a teacher,"* insists John. *"He was my team-mate and I was happy to share what I knew. In fact, I treated him more like a little brother."* The perfect understanding between the two men did not prevent the younger man from giving the older one a hard time, right from the start of battle.

6th in Argentina, 5th in Brazil, having dispensed with Riccardo Patrese, who had a reputation for being tough to pass, Alain Prost had passed his Grand Prix entry exam with flying colours. On top of that, he clearly dominated his team-mate in qualifying. The public and the press discovered a new talent, while he instantly became a big hit with the McLaren team, to the detriment of poor Watson, which actually irritated Alain. The Frenchman was therefore in confident mood as he prepared to tackle the third round in South Africa. But after qualifying, he returned from hospital in Johannesburg with his arm in plaster and Watson as his driver and nurse. A suspension component had broken at full speed and the M29B hit the barriers very hard. Alain was worried for two reasons: his broken wrist meant

John Watson: "Alain seemed to be born in the McLaren"

A Formula 1 driver from 1973, John Watson won the 1976 Austrian Grand Prix at the wheel of a Penske, before driving for Brabham and then McLaren. So he was professionally qualified to cast a keen eye over Alain Prost's debut in Formula 1, when he tested at Paul Ricard in November 1979. He remembers:

"Kevin drove first. It was immediately obvious to me that this represented an opportunity not to be missed. I noticed a few small details such as the way he accelerated and went up and down the gearbox. I reckon he was nervous. Then Alain got behind the wheel and I saw a different person; someone who drove smoothly and seemed perfectly at ease in a Formula 1 car. Even the guys in the pits noticed it. He handled the power well and seemed born in the car! He made it look so easy. I think he adapted his driving style to the new car very quickly. He braked and changed gear well and it seemed he was not pushing himself over his limit as it was all very natural. He had a fantastic pace! It was obvious to everyone present that day that he was in a different league to Kevin. I was not involved in choosing the driver for the following year but it was clear that Alain had an enormous potential to make it in Formula 1."

● **37**_In the McLaren camp, Bruno Giacomelli had been nicknamed "Jack O'Malley," while John Watson was referred to as "John What's wrong," because he often complained about his car. Alain's nickname was based on his diminutive stature and his nationality as seen by the British (visible on the bodywork.) Then, when the Frenchman ended up with his arm in a sling after his Kyalami accident, the mechanics renamed him "Napoleon."

P. MÉNARD

Designer: Gordon Coppuck

Engine

Make/Type: Ford Cosworth DFV
Number of Cylinders/Configuration: V8 (Front and Rear)
Capacity: 2993 cc
Bore/Stroke: 85.6 x 64.8 mm
Compression ratio: 12:1
Maximum power: 470 hp
Maximum revs: 10800 rpm
Block material: Aluminium
Fuel/Oil: Castrol
Sparking plugs: Champion
Injection: Lucas
Valve gear: 4 ACT
Number of valves per cylinder: 4
Ignition: Lucas Contactless
Weight: 163 kg

Transmission

Gearbox/Number of gears: McLaren Hewland (5)
Clutch: Borg & Beck

Chassis

Type : Aluminium monocoque
Suspension: Upper arms with pendulum, lower wishbones, inboard
Front and Rear springs
Shock absorbers: Koni
Rim diameter: 13" and 15" (Front) / 15" (Rear)
Rim width: 11" (Front) / 16" and 18" (Rear)
Tyres: Goodyear
Brakes: Lockheed

Dimensions

Wheelbase: 2743 mm
Track: 1727 mm (Front) / 1574 mm (Rear)
Dry weight: 600 kg
Fuel capacity: 177 litres

Raced from Argentina to Austria.

he could not take part in the race, nor in the next round at Long Beach, but above all, the accident raised doubts about the quality of the car he was driving. Earlier, in the morning, he had already been off the track for the same reason, fortunately without injury.

The flashy brilliance at the start of the season was already a distant memory. Prost now mistrusted his equipment and worried about the way the team was run by Teddy Mayer, who seemed to ignore the young driver's alarmist remarks. In testing at Donington, the same suspension failure reoccurred and Alain injured his cervical vertebrae. Events in Spain were to really alert him to the dangers of driving a bad car. *"This car really gave me the shivers,"* he recalls with a retrospective shudder! *"At Jarama, it had new front suspension, riveted to the monocoque. Going down the "Bugatti Esses" which led into the bowl behind the pits, the suspension broke the first time I braked hard and*

the two front wheels flew off! The GPDA (Grand Prix Drivers Association) had only just insisted on having a large run off with catch fencing as there had been nothing there before. So I went straight on and it felt as though I was heading straight into the paddock. Luckily it dug in at the back, which spun me around. But for that I think I would have been killed!" This time, it was not just the suspension that broke: Prost's confidence and morale were also damaged. A driver needs blind faith in his equipment and his team to attack without hesitation. It is one of the basic laws of mechanised sports. But at that point, at the start of the summer of 1980, Alain Prost had lost faith in his team. He took some consolation in the growing rumours that Marlboro were not happy with the way Teddy Mayer ran the team and was that the sponsor was really keen on replacing him with Ron Dennis, who brought with him a revolutionary technology thought up by designer John Barnard. Keen not to lose such a

• **38**_"You see, it's the wrist that's broken – I see." In South Africa, coming out of hospital, Alain Prost shows the X-rays of his injured wrist to a member of the team. "Napoleon" would have to sit out the next two Grands Prix and would thus have plenty of time to reflect on the integrity of the McLaren. In twenty years of racing at the highest level, it was to be the most serious injury Alain Prost ever had to complain about!

talent, the two men even invited him to take a look at the Project Four workshops over the summer. They explained their vision of the future, showing him the mock up of the new car, although they did not reveal all its secrets. Prost was impressed by Dennis' personality and by Barnard's serious approach, but asked for time to think. For some time now, Gérard Larrousse had hinted to Alain that he wanted him to join Renault, alongside René Arnoux for 1981. The scales were finely balanced: on the one side British pragmatism and a mouth-watering project, on the other, the excitement and pride of finally driving for a French team with, as a plus, the famous turbo engine. Alain therefore waited for the slightest difference that would tip the scales one way or the other. On Friday, 1st August, a few days after taking a hard fought sixth place in the British Grand Prix, Alain Prost married Anne-Marie Barges, with whom he moved into a small apartment he had recently bought in Saint-

Chamond with his first McLaren pay cheques, not far from the rue Dugas-Montbel, which he left with some regret. They had two boys, Nicolas in 1981 and Sacha in 1990. The wedding day should have been a great celebration but in the afternoon news came through like a thunderbolt that Patrick Depailler, whom Alain had grown close to, had just been killed in private testing at Hockenheim at the wheel of an Alfa Romeo. This tragedy revived the ever present doubts about the handling of the McLaren for the young man.

A new car, the M30 made its debut in Holland. Prost found it to be an improvement, especially in terms of stiffness and finished sixth in the Grand Prix. He began to harbour hopes that thing were on the up within the team, especially as John Barnard was now in regular attendance and it seemed the team's future lay in a takeover by Ron Dennis. In Canada, John Watson finally clicked out of his losing streak and he and Alain were fighting for third place when

• **39**_Relations did not improve during the course of the season between Alain Prost and Teddy Mayer. The team boss would not listen to the questions from his driver about the design of the cars, preferring to keep an ear to the ground when it came to what Marlboro was up to.

the suspension broke yet again on the Frenchman's car. It was a disappointment that turned to bitterness when a rear wishbone broke during practice in the United States. The car buried itself under the barrier and a wheel dealt Prost's helmet a heavy blow. He was rushed to the circuit medical centre and Watson hurried off to see him. *"I was the first to see Alain in the medical centre and he said to me, 'John, next year you will be number one at McLaren, because I will never drive for them again."*

Alain had severe pains in his head and naturally scratched from the race, packed his bags and caught the first flight for France. *"I was bedridden for two weeks. I had to lean against the wall to get to the toilet. I had lost some vision in the left eye. And that is what made opt in favour of Renault. At the time, even Marlboro did not insist on changing my mind as they saw that it was more than a purely sporting matter. They understood and almost helped me leave. In fact I was still a Marlboro driver when I went to Renault."* However, Teddy Mayer was not so ready to lose his "find" and waved the contract signed by Alain, which stated he was tied to the team for three years. The Frenchman admitted to signing the document, but pointed out that the team he had signed for no longer existed. He was right as, on 1st November, Team McLaren had been transformed into McLaren International and that its real boss was now Ron Dennis. ∎

• **40**_When the new M30 arrived in Holland, things seemed to improve and Alain scrabbled his way to another point in Zandvoort. But it still had structural problems and only the arrival of Ron Dennis and John Barnard at the end of the year eased the situation. But by then, Prost had decided to go and experience the joys of the turbo.

P. MÉNARD

Designer: Gordon Coppuck

Same technical caracteristics then M29B/C, except:

Dimensions
Wheelbase: 2692 mm
Track: 1752 mm (Front) / 1600 mm (Rear)

Raced from Netherland to United States
(Even though Prost withdraw from the United States GP).

Chapter 8
1981-1982
Return of the
Renault prodigal

● **42**_1981 Argentinian
Grand Prix. Alain Prost (no.
15) starts at the wheel of the
Renault RE20B surrounded
by future rivals with plenty of
experience, Nelson Piquet in
the Brabham (no. 5) and Alan
Jones in the Williams (no. 1.)
Carlos Reutemann is just
behind.

At the end of 1980, Alain and Gérard Larrousse signed a contract in Renault's offices in Boulogne Billancourt tying the driver to Renault-Sport. His fame was still at the embryonic stage in France and only the real enthusiasts knew he had enjoyed a great debut season with McLaren, given the problems he had experienced. Alain was conscious of the fact he now had the right equipment to make his mark. Having entered Formula 1 in 1977 with the new and complex turbocharging technology, Renault had been winning races for the past two years. The cars were quick, but suffered a cruel lack of mechanical reliability. He knew therefore that a lot of development and fine tuning work lay ahead of him. On top of that, he knew absolutely nothing about the workings of a turbocharged engine.

Right from the very first test session at the Paul Ricard circuit, buffeted by an icy cold Mistral winter wind, Alain Prost discovered the RS20B that had been raced in 1980. Impressed by the power of the turbo engine, he did not push too hard, simply trying to drive as neatly as possible. He found the car to be very heavy compared with the McLaren - there was an 80 kg difference! - but he soon settled into the job of getting the

most out of it. Unfortunately, his new team-mate, René Arnoux, did not take long to realise what was going on. The first major test session of the 1981 season took place in Buenos Aires and Arnoux, appeared to festering with a pernicious depression. He had driven for Renault since 1979 and had won twice in 1980, but the little new-boy kept sticking it to him by a second a lap! All Grand Prix drivers will tell you that their most dangerous rival is their team-mate as he is the only one to share identical equipment, the only one with whom to make a direct comparison. Every driver therefore tries to get the psychological upper hand over their team-mate by whatever means possible. After John Watson, it was now René Arnoux's turn to be taken apart and before the season had even begun! The imperceptible but insidious germ of discord was already in place, especially as the pecking order of the two men was not seen the same way within the team. Alain tells a revealing anecdote on this point: *"At McLaren, when you arrived in the morning, everyone shouted out 'good morning' and in the evening there was a round of 'have a good night, see you in the morning.' In the Renault camp, at the first test, I had to shake everyone by the hand, as René did it to everyone,* both morning and night. I didn't, having got into the English habit by this time. I thought it wasn't important, but I realised it was frowned on. For me, it was bordering on a waste of time and efficiency rather than a courtesy. The team members go their own way at six in the evening and are back together again the next morning. If you have to go through this type of thing every time, it causes problems. I think the English have a better handle on it." It might be just a small detail, but it speaks volumes about the evolution of Alain's way of thinking. It goes some way to explaining the problems he would always encounter with Latin culture and especially the French. Although he was not fully aware of the fact at the time, he had already espoused the English mentality when it came to work. When he later attempted to take on a national challenge, the devil was in this type of detail and, along with other difficulties, contributed to his failure. He was sure that Arnoux had a more convivial image and that even the general public was unconsciously swayed by this. It would also have an effect on Prost's image as an undoubted champion who would never be a prophet in his own land.

Apart from this anodyne irritant, Alain Prost delighted his team. His analytical powers and his smooth driving style blended in perfectly with the brutality of the turbo engine. It was an example to others. One of the turbo engine's characteristics was a relative lack of engine braking compared to a normally aspirated engine and so the brakes came in for a hard time. Even in this area, Alain was always kinder to the equipment than his team-mate. It was a trait that stuck with him throughout his career. Prost developed a reputation for getting his car to the chequered flag in better condition than the majority of his peers.

But in stark contrast to the reputation that preceded him, Prost got the 1981 championship underway with a silly accident that saw him crash into the barriers at Long Beach at the start of practice, before tangling with the fiery Andrea de Cesaris at the start of the race! In Brazil, he was harpooned by Didier Pironi's out of control Ferrari and so it was not until Argentina that the little Frenchman was able to produce a well thought out drive to third place. It was the first of 104 podium finishes!

Unfortunately, this good showing was followed by a string of four retirements, three of them down to mechanical failure on the new RE30, which still lacked reliability. Coming up to the half-season and the French Grand Prix, Alain still only had his 4 points from Argentina, while René was on 2. Let's say there were some worried faces in the yellow and black camp and that a good result on home turf would be a welcome

Bernard Dudot: "He would think before getting in the car"

Architect of the Renault V6 turbo project, which included Endurance and F1, in the Seventies and technical director of the Renault team from 1980, Bernard Dudot has appreciated Alain Prost's development abilities since 1981:
"He had his very own way of fine tuning a car. He took a long time to set meaningful lap times because, as part of his own reference points at any given track, he would improve the car point by point, chassis, tyres, suspension engine etcetera. He would get his reference points corner by corner and when during a lap he felt that he had found the right compromise, he would then string together a lap time that surprised everyone. He would wait until the car was just right before attacking the lap, unlike other drivers who just go for a time from the off. Alain began by thinking, to work out the cars attributes and defects, gradually making improvements until he would go for a time. And when he did, that lap time was truly representative of what the car could do.
For us, it was an interesting source of information as we could rely on that time being an optimum for the car. But a driver who pushes the car to its limits right away does not provide reliable responses as we don't know which way to go from there. René was much more intuitive, if I can say that and he was quick. If things were going well, the car would soon be performing well, but if things were more difficult, he would just clam up which was a bit of a disaster for the team."

Designer: Renault Sport Design Team

Engine

Make/Type: Renault EF1
Number of Cylinders/Configuration: V6 (Rear)
Capacity: 1492 cc
Bore/Stroke: 86 x 42.8 mm
Compression ratio: 6.8:1
Turbo(s): 2, KKK
Maximum power: 560 hp
Maximum revs: 11500 rpm
Block material: Aluminium
Fuel/Oil: Elf
Sparking plugs: Champion
Injection: Bosch-Kugelfischer
Valve gear: 4 ACT
Number of valves per cylinder: 4
Ignition: Magneti Marelli
Weight (without intercoolers): 180 kg

Transmission

Gearbox/Number of gears: Hewland FGA 400 (5)
Clutch: AP

Chassis

Type: Aluminium monocoque
Suspension: Upper arms with pendulum, lower wishbones, inboard
Front and Rear springs
Shock absorbers: Koni
Rim diameter: 13" (Front and Rear)
Rim width: 9.5" (Front) / 16.5" (Rear)
Tyres: Michelin
Brakes: AP

Dimensions

Wheelbase: 2860 mm
Track: 1706 mm (Front) / 1531 mm (Rear)
Dry weight: 615 kg
Fuel capacity: 225 litres

Raced from Long Beach (United States West) to San Marino.

morale booster. In qualifying, the Renaults had finally come good and René took pole position, while Alain was third. Much of the improvement was due to the soft Michelin tyres that were much better than the Goodyear qualifiers. But in the race, the Akron rubber proved superior and Alain could nothing but follow a long way behind race leader Nelson Piquet and his Brabham for 58 laps, a task made all the more difficult as, by this point, he could no longer engage fourth gear. At that point, a terrific storm hit the Dijon-Prenois circuit and the clerk of the course brought out the red flag. While waiting for the restart, the Renault mechanics tried feverishly to fix the gearbox. When the skies brightened and the race was about to start again, they had to bolt it back together having failed to sort the problem. There were 22 laps to go. With such a short distance, Michelin's technical director Pierre Dupasquier maintained that the soft tyres would last to the end and so they were fitted to the

RE30. Piquet was scowling, knowing the race was all but lost. Indeed, Alain shot off into the lead at the second start and then, a miracle! He suddenly found fourth gear again! The rest was just a formality for the 26 year old who thus took his first ever Formula 1 win. Apart from the obvious delight, Prost soon discovered the other benefits of his performance: *"The first win grants you access to the privileged Grand Prix winners club. Psychologically, it changes your perspective. Every time you roll up to the start, even if you are a long way back, you think you can win. Before, it was impossible to think like that."*

From then on, Alain Prost would always be a frontrunner and some observers already had him marked down as a world champion in the making. He won two more grands prix that summer, in Zandvoort and Monza, but what marked him out was his level headed approach in only his second season of Formula 1. In Germany, having to cope with an engine that was losing power, he switched to a very aggressive style to hang onto second place behind Piquet. In Holland, he got the upper hand in his mano a mano with the reigning world champion, the robust Alan Jones and it was one of the best drives of his career. It was this race that earned Prost the nickname of "the professor." His understanding and ability when it came to choosing tyres was already well known and it was knowing how to look after them that allowed him to close on Jones in Zandvoort. In Montreal, in a downpour, he was in a class of his own in the lead, before being stupidly pushed off the track by a novice Nigel Mansell who had forgotten to indicate before turning! Alain finished the 1981 season in style, with a second place in Las Vegas, which put him fifth in the championship with three wins, the same number as the new world champion, Nelson Piquet and more than any other winners that year. It has to be said that but for the constant mechanical failures, Prost would have been in the hunt for the title fair and square. But that's motor racing and at least a new star was born and a young champion was on his way, as far the general public was concerned.

Indeed, the majority of racing pundits made Alain Prost and Renault favourites to take the titles in 1982. In the second half of the 1981 season, the French team demonstrated that it had resolved its reliability problems and its star driver had taken only a year to go from being a young hopeful to potential champion. Logic demanded that this team had everything in place to emerge victorious. However, fate would unfortunately play its part.

The 1982 season would definitely go down as one of the worst, if not the worst in the Formula 1 world champion's career. It was a year packed with human drama, discord and endless politics which rendered it rotten to the core. Alain would taste his fair share of bitterness and sadness this year. All the same, it got off to a good start with a superb win at Kyalami (see next chapter,) followed by a second victory in Rio, that came to him in the courts a few weeks later after the first two, Piquet and Rosberg had been disqualified. The pundits looked to have got it right. Renault and Prost were outrageously dominant in the early stages of the championship. Eight rounds later, on the night of the British Grand Prix, the driver and his team

• **44**_The 1981 French Grand Prix was run in two parts because of a storm. As soon as the sun reappeared, Prost took the lead ahead of Watson, Arnoux and Piquet, thanks to his soft Michelin tyres and the miraculous return of 4th gear. It was his first Formula 1 win.

had slipped to fifth place in both classifications. In eight races, Renault had only managed to score ONE point, thanks to Alain's sixth place at Brands Hatch! Apart from Monaco, where Prost was leading until he made the mistake of hitting the barrier towards the end of the race when he was still going flat out, the whole fiasco was down to a succession of mechanical failures.

Prost was less in a rage about the failures themselves than he was about their cause, which he felt could have been avoided. Since 1981, Bernard Dudot and his engine specialists, including Jean-Pierre Boudy had tried to improve the driveability of the V6 and to increase its power band. They finally sorted out an injection system driven by a small electric motor. In terms of performance, the new design brought a

substantial gain which no one, especially Alain, ever thought to question. The problem stemmed from the little electric motor, modified by Renault, which kept shaking itself to bits because of the vibrations. *"The little Renix motor which drove the electronic injection broke all the time,"* recalls Alain. *"We also had a Marelli unit that we used from time to time in practice and which had done kilometre after kilometre without any problem. But "someone" high up had said we had to use the Renix. I retired a few times during the year because of it. Looking back, you have to say it was a real waste."* This failure occurred in Austria and Italy when he could still have entertained some hopes for the title. Aware of the malaise, Boudy ordered a reliable motor from an aeronautical company, but it arrived at the

1981 French Grand Prix
Renault RE30

P.MÉNARD

Designer: Renault Sport Design Team

Engine
Make/Type: Renault EF1
Number of Cylinders/Configuration: V6 (Rear)
Capacity: 1492 cc
Bore/Stroke: 86 x 42.8 mm
Compression ratio: 6.8:1
Turbo(s): 2, KKK
Maximum power: 560 hp
Maximum revs: 11500 rpm
Block material: Aluminium
Fuel/Oil: Elf
Sparking plugs: Champion
Injection: Bosch-Kugelfischer
Valve gear: 4 ACT
Number of valves per cylinder: 4
Ignition: Magneti Marelli
Weight (without intercoolers): 180 kg

Transmission
Gearbox/Number of gears: Renault type 30-Hewland (5)
Clutch: AP

Chassis
Type: Monocoque en aluminium
Suspension: Upper arms with pendulum, lower wishbones, inboard Front and Rear springs
Shock absorbers: Koni
Rim diameter: 13" (Front and Rear)
Rim width: 9.5" (Front) / 16.5" (Rear)
Tyres: Michelin
Brakes: AP

Dimensions
Wheelbase: 2730 mm
Track: 1740 mm (Front) / 1630 mm (Rear)
Dry weight: 605 kg
Fuel capacity: 225 litres

Raced from Belgium to Las Vegas.

end of the season. Today, Bernard Dudot can only regret these mistakes which can be put down to management. *"It was Renault-Sport's decision that was prejudicial in this affair, as it chose a piece of equipment that was not adapted to the environment and the demands of a Formula 1 car. But the team was too young and was in the process of coming together, so people were still learning. Basically, we were just too inexperienced."* Added to errors of technical management were errors of man management.

Although all seemed calm from the outside, the cohabitation between Prost and Arnoux became more and more tense with every passing race. In Monaco, Alain accused René of having blocked him in qualifying but Arnoux was finding it ever more difficult to deal with the

authoritarian attitude of his team-mate. Even though Alain was still in the running for the championship, René, who was out of the title race, refused to budge. After an admirable demonstration of efficiency at the French Grand Prix with Arnoux and Prost on the front row, Gérard Larrousse came up with tactics aimed at luring Renault's most dangerous opposition, the Brabhams of Piquet and Patrese into a well thought out trap. Larrousse suggested that René should take off like a hare with more turbo boost, hoping that the two British cars would try and follow and break as a consequence. At that point, Arnoux was expected to meekly move over and let his team leader keep his championship hopes alive. René accepted the deal. On lap 23 of 54, Nelson Piquet parked his Brabham with a dead

engine and Larrousse's plan had worked, with the two Renaults now out in front. René led Alain by 10 seconds, while Prost was 16 seconds ahead of Pironi's Ferrari. The pit board "Alain 1 – René 2" was duly shown to the leader, who decided to ignore it! Arnoux had done his sums. For over a year he had lived by Prost's law and had experienced moments of terrible doubt. He had not won since Brazil in 1980 and here was the smell of victory once again in his nose. He was expected to ignore it for the sake of some mathematical reasons worked out by the factory and that meant little to him. *"René drove for pleasure, Alain drove to be world champion,"* recalled Pierre Dupasquier recently. Pleasure had to be sated and René would not back off. On the podium, the contrast between the expressions said it all. While Pironi seemed pretty satisfied with his third place that strengthened his hold on the championship and Arnoux sprayed the champagne in triumph, Prost looked the way he had done five years earlier on the Pau podium. This time, there was no Marc Cerneau around to tell him to smile and the fans could see for themselves the mood he was in. Although the young driver's achievements were appreciated for what they were in his home country, the French always found it difficult to take national pride in this rather cold, calculating and pragmatic lad. They prefered the bonhomie and natural warmth of someone like Arnoux, even if he was less diligent in his approach at every race. They say the French have always had a penchant for those

who come second, as in cycling where they loved Poulidor but disdained Anquetil. They also have an irritating tendency to burn their idols as soon as they have turned to gold. This wave of rejection was to sting Prost like a whiplash and the scars would affect him for a long time, as he is more sensitive than one would think. *"I did not really have it in for René,"* Prost is keen to point out. *"That, despite the fact he did not keep his word. I can even understand that it was difficult for him to move aside, especially in the French Grand Prix. I did object to being seen as a bad loser. People form an opinion on what they have seen and there was no way they could understand that one driver would be asked to move over for another. Given that the team bosses do not explain what they have done, the public cannot understand. I do not bear him a grudge, but I suffered a lot because of it over the years."* Indeed, we will see later than when the image is tarnished, the scars can open again.

As mentioned earlier, 1982 was a sinister year from a human point of view. In Montreal, young Riccardo Paletti buried his Osella into the back of Didier Pironi's Ferrari as they left the grid. The Italian debutant was killed on the spot. A few weeks earlier, it had been Gilles Villeneuve, the seemingly indestructible tightrope walker who lost his life in a brutal accident at Zolder. Alain was personally affected. He appreciated the Canadian's joyously simple approach to life and admired his spectacular driving style. When Didier Pironi's Ferrari slammed into him full pelt in the fog of rain that hung over Hockenheim on the Saturday afternoon of qualifying for the German Grand Prix, Alain Prost began to question his very existence.

Leading the championship and on provisional pole after the previous day's dry qualifying, Pironi attacked majestically in the early afternoon of 7th August on a soaking track, as if to underline his psychological superiority. Travelling flat out down the straight leading back to the Stadium section, he sensed rather than saw Derek Daly's Williams move to one side. Alain recalls the painful incident. *"I thing they* (Daly and Pironi) *were doing about 250 km/h. Daly passed me on the right and, blinded by the spray, Didier thought he was letting him past and accelerated in a straight line. I didn't see it coming because there was a lot of water. You have to understand that at Hockenheim, when it rains the spray hangs in the air for ten or fifteen seconds after a car has thrown it up. The Ferrari flew as high as the trees and it passed over me with a rushing noise. It fell down rear end first and in the impact that followed it broke again at the front. My car had no brakes, but I managed to stop. I went over to Didier, but...(silence) they are terrible memories. These are things you have no control over that you cannot dominate. It stayed with me, it stopped me."* Pironi had terrible leg injuries and only just avoided amputation. His Formula 1 career ended that day, but sadly he was killed in an offshore powerboat race in 1987. Back in the motorhome, Alain's face was riddled with doubt and retrospective fear. He sincerely considered packing it in. It took all Gérard Larrousse's powers of persuasion to get him back in the car before fear took over forever. But lack of visibility in the rain would always be synonymous with danger and Alain decided never again to take uncontrolled risks in these

• **46**_By taking his third grand prix victory of the 1981 season in Italy, Alain Prost set a record for a French driver and became a true champion. Certainly his Renault mechanics believed that to be the case.
(Anne Boisnard Archive)

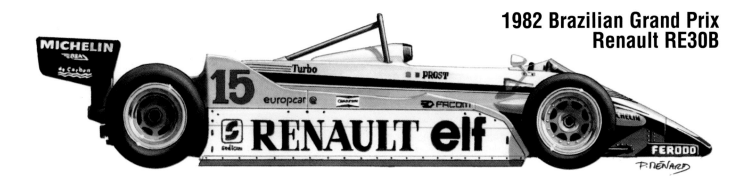

P. NÉNARD

Designer: Renault Sport

Dimensions
Wheelbase: 1730 mm (Front) / 1655 mm (Rear)
Dry weight: 600 kg

Same technical caracteristics then R30, except:

Used all season.

• **47**_The Grand Prix of discord: René Arnoux (no 16) had agreed to let Alain Prost (no 15) through into the lead in the closing stages. Finally, he could not bring himself to do it and won the event much to the fury of his team-mate, who had it in for the instigators of this trickery.

conditions. This attitude can be seen as the reason for his pulling out at Silverstone in 1988 and Adelaide in 1989, although different causes were put forward at the time.

Although he finished the championship one place higher up the order than the previous year, Prost still has bitter memories of the 1982 season. He knew that he and his team missed a clear opportunity to take the title and hoped that all would be put right in 1983 and that the team would not repeat the mistakes of the past. In order to achieve this goal, he asked to be more involved in technical decisions and to be

consulted over the choice of his next team-mate, given that Arnoux had signed for Ferrari. Eddie Cheever, the young Italian-American seemed appropriate as he was a quick driver and a nice guy. At the end of a troubled season, Alain decided on a change of scenery and in October, he took part in the Rallye du Var (see below.) Then, in November, he flew to Calder, Australia to race in a Formula Pacific event, a sort of more powerful version of Formula 3. Along with a few good mates, he made the most of enjoying himself, but back on track, instinct took over and after taking pole, he won the race! ∎

Eyewitness account of Dany Snobeck: "Alain was far from ridiculous"

Like all drivers of the modern F1 era, Alain Prost concentrated exclusively on single-seaters during his long racing career. In October 1982, he veered off that track to try his hand at the joys of rallying. He chose the Rallye du Var, driving an R5 Turbo prepared by his friend Dany Snobeck who recalls the way Alain tackled the event:

"His approach was very professional. We prepared cars for Renault, whom he represented in Formula 1. He wanted to try a rally and so it was natural he would chose to do so in one of our cars. He took on one of the best co-drivers at the time, the late Jean-Marc Andrie (who died a few years ago.) He turned up ten days ahead of the event despite his busy schedule. He put all he had into it, always asking for advice and he tried the car a lot. He came to the factory, tried out seats, leaving no avenue unexplored. He prepared himself as though he was tackling a world championship event. He certainly wasn't there just to have a laugh! Some say he did not feel comfortable in the car, but I am not convinced. You have to remember he had stepped out of a Formula 1 car and that's completely different. Take any current F1 driver, would any of them be comfortable in a rally car? He was in the top five. At the time, Jean-Marc Andrié admitted to me that he had been very surprised at how well Alain had adapted. He's a guy who knows how to drive and who has the talent. I reckon that if he had continued rallying he would have surprised a few people. He was not ridiculous in the event, but it ended when he crashed out because of a stupid problem when the throttle jammed open."

• **48**_Alain Prost and Dany Snobeck listen to Jean-Marc Andrié during a night stage on the 1982 Rallye du Var. *(Dany Snobeck archives)*

• **49**_The Swiss Grand Prix held at the Dijon-Prenois circuit at the end of the season represented Prost's last chance to grab the world title crown. A damaged skirt and an on-form Keke Rosberg at the end of the race robbed him of his final hopes of glory.

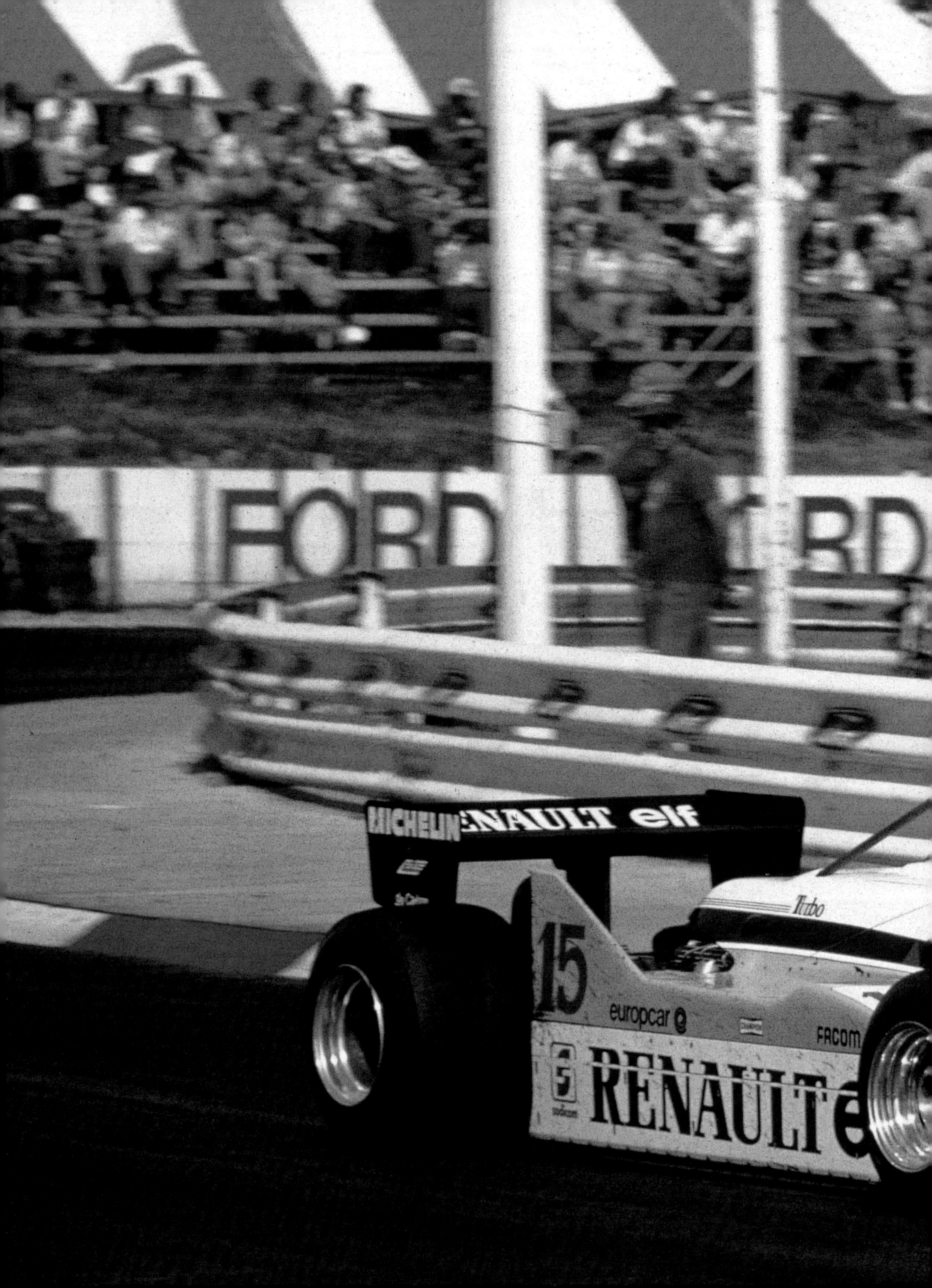
FORD
MICHELIN
elf
Turbo
15
europcar
FACOM
RENAULT

Chapter 9
A golden puncture

"A memorable race"
South African Grand Prix
23rd January 1982

Before we tackle the third episode in Alain Prost's peregrination within the heart of the Renault team, let us take a look at one of his most sensational races, which furthermore would also have important consequences in terms of the evolution of Grand Prix racing. The 1982 championship got off to an astounding start as the drivers united against the iniquitous and unilateral decision taken by the FISA and the constructors, which pretty much said that a driver could not leave his team when he wanted, but on the contrary, a team could get rid of a driver whenever it felt like it. Shocked but determined, all these egocentric individuals somehow got together and staged a strike, something which had never been seen before or since in the annals of Formula 1. For the sake of unity, they made their headquarters in the main lounge of a hotel some distance from the track. *"The Kyalami strike remains one of my favourite memories in terms of the atmosphere between the drivers,"* recalls Alain with evident enjoyment. *"There were some amazing moments like the piano duo between Villeneuve and De Angelis and we were all sleeping on camp beds. Then Giacomelli – now there was a character – had given us a "lesson in terrorism," with him at the blackboard and the rest of us sitting down like school kids. He showed us how to make a bomb and everything and we were dying laughing! You cannot imagine anything like that happening these days. I really miss the characters and the personalities from those days."* Finally, an agreement was reached between the drivers and the governing body, just in time for a shortened qualifying and the race. As the season was only just getting underway, one had to rely on hearsay when it came to working out the likely hierarchy for the coming season and what it might have in store. As we have seen previously, Alain and Renault were heavily backed for the

title race, with the most likely threat coming from the Ferraris of Villeneuve and Pironi, the Brabham-BMW of reigning champion Nelson Piquet, his new team-mate, Riccardo Patrese, the Williams-Fords of Carlos Reutemann and Keke Rosberg and, who knows, maybe the reborn McLaren-Fords of John Watson and the returning Niki Lauda who was making a comeback having taken two years off to run his airline business. As for the first Grand Prix, it was clear that only the turbo engines would be on the pace at this altitude. That is indeed what happened as the top six cars in qualifying were all supercharged. René Arnoux took pole with ease, while Alain could do no better than fifth, having had to switch to his T-car when he had a heavy crash following a puncture. It was to be only the first.

At the green light, Arnoux shot off into the lead and Prost made the perfect start to run just behind his team-mate into the first braking area. Piquet nearly stalled as he let the clutch out, as he was not really used to the turbo, Patrese made an awful start and that left Pironi to come through to third place, followed by Villeneuve. All these good people were soon to retire. Piquet missed a braking point, Patrese and Villeneuve suffered broken turbos, while Pironi slipped down the order to finish...18th! The Renaults charged off ahead without anyone to worry about and Alain passed René on lap 13. He was thus in the lead on a track he did not know particularly well, considering that his 1980 race was cut short and that the previous day's qualifying had been very brief. Nevertheless, he felt comfortable, controlling the race and enjoying the flow of fast corners which required a very smooth driving style. Attacking lap 39, he felt the car suddenly break away from him. He just managed to catch it, slowed down and worked out that the problem was caused by a left rear puncture! *"The problem was that it came right at the start of*

the lap. So I had to bring the car back to the pits slowly so as to do as little damage as possible to the car. In this type of situation, the tendency is to drive a bit too quickly. At the time, the cars had skirts which needed to be looked after." Having completed lap 40 at a slow pace, he rolled down pit lane, the car running on its left rear rim. The side pod was damaged, but there was nothing to be done about it and Alain rejoined the track going like a rocket, with four new tyres and a grim determination. He was running eighth, one lap down. No one took much notice of Renault no. 15 from then on, as it had no chance of winning. How wrong could they be?

Thinking it through, Prost told himself that a few points would come in useful for this championship that had only just begun. But he immediately realised that his car was still running perfectly and that a podium finish might yet be on the cards. He knuckled down and so began what would always be one of his greatest fight-backs. Having disposed of Alboreto's Tyrrell,

he dealt with the two McLarens of Lauda and Watson and, on lap 55, passed Rosberg for fourth place. He set the fastest race lap and began to close on Reutemann, before overwhelming Pironi on lap 62. Those who liked to keep a lap chart could not believe their eyes. Alain Prost was now second and putting pressure on Arnoux, whose tyres were suffering. The incredible happened on lap 68 of 77. Renault no. 15 dealt with no. 16 as if it was not there!

Alain went on to win as he pleased, with a 15 second lead over Carlos Reutemann, who passed Arnoux on the last lap. Warmly congratulated by his team, he stepped onto the podium looking fresh as a daisy. Somewhere in the crowd, Brabham technical director, Gordon Murray was thinking about what he had just witnessed. *"At the time, there were no pit stops,"* recalls Alain. *"And it was my situation that gave Gordon Murray the idea of planning pit stops into the race strategy, as he confided to me later. In fact, I would have won the race anyway, but the mishap made it all the more enjoyable."* ■

● **51**_Right from the start, the two Renaults shot off into a dominant lead. Alain was soon to pass René and comfortably increase his lead with every passing lap, up to lap 39.

● **52**_This shows the state of Prost's car when he pitted on lap 40! One can clearly see the damage caused to the vertical barge board at the back of the left side pod and one of the wheel men ready to spring into action. Most of the observers assumed the Frenchman was now out of the running.

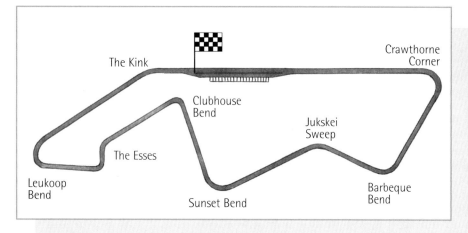

KYALAMI, THE CIRCUIT
Permanent circuit
4.104 km / 2.550 miles

Situated 25 km from the centre of Johannesburg at an altitude of 1500 metres in the high plains of the surrounding area, the circuit of Kyalami (it means "at my place" in Swahili) was built in 1961, in a project managed by the South African Motor Racing Club. By the end of that year, races were staged, the most famous being the "9 Hours of Kyalami" which was a cornerstone of the Endurance championship for many years. At the start of the Sixties, South Africa welcomed the Formula 1 World Championship at the East London circuit on the Indian Ocean. In order to test and to make the long trip financially viable, several teams had got in the habit of turning up at Kyalami a week before the race to take part in the non-championship Rand Grand Prix. Which is why the list of winners at that circuit included the likes of Jim Clark, John Surtees and Graham Hill.

In 1967, the ageing East London track was abandoned in favour of Kyalami, so most of the drivers found themselves back on familiar terrain. The track layout was very fast, with a very long and wide main straight that climbed from Leukopp Bend to the start-finish line, before dropping down to Crawthorne, with the straight broken by Kink corner, which was taken flat. The difficulty of the circuit lay in the compromise between having the right amount of aerodynamic downforce to deal with the flowing section from Barbeque Bend to Leukoop Bend, without losing out through too much drag reducing top speed that was so important down the pit straight. From 1967 to 1985, the layout remained unchanged and Mexico's Pedro Rodriguez was the first winner in his Cooper-Maserati. The racing-mad South African fans were delighted to see their local boy, Jody Scheckter, win the 1975 Grand Prix in a Tyrrell, but they also had to deal with the tragedies of the death of Peter Revson in 1974 and Tom Pryce in 1977. Jim Clark took his 25th and final Grand Prix win here in 1968 and Niki Lauda holds the record for most wins with three, in 1976, 1977 and 1984. In 1981, the Grand Prix was a non-championship event with only the FOCA teams taking part, without Renault, Ferrari, Alfa Romeo and Ligier. So, when Alain Prost arrived at Kyalami in 1982, his only memory of the place was the painful one of his accident in the Esses in 1980.

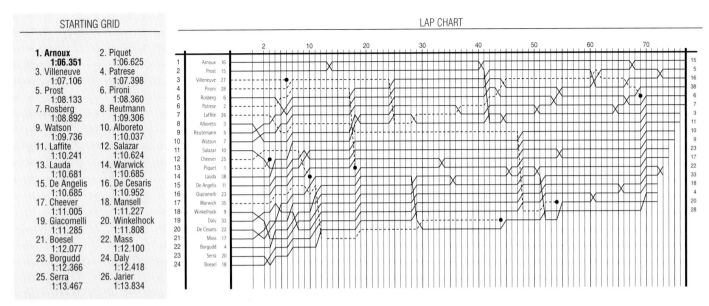

STARTING GRID

1. Arnoux **1:06.351**	2. Piquet 1:06.625
3. Villeneuve 1:07.106	4. Patrese 1:07.398
5. Prost 1:08.133	6. Pironi 1:08.360
7. Rosberg 1:08.892	8. Reutmann 1:09.306
9. Watson 1:09.736	10. Alboreto 1:10.037
11. Laffite 1:10.241	12. Salazar 1:10.624
13. Lauda 1:10.681	14. Warwick 1:10.685
15. De Angelis 1:10.685	16. De Cesaris 1:10.952
17. Cheever 1:11.005	18. Mansell 1:11.227
19. Giacomelli 1:11.285	20. Winkelhock 1:11.808
21. Boesel 1:12.077	22. Mass 1:12.100
23. Borgudd 1:12.366	24. Daly 1:12.418
25. Serra 1:13.467	26. Jarier 1:13.834

LAP CHART

• 53_Not even tired! After a fantastic fight-back from 8th to 1st, Alain sprays the champagne in lively fashion to celebrate a weekend where he really had some fun.

RESULTS - 77 race laps for 316.008 km

1. Prost	**Renault**	**77**	**1:32:08.401** **205.779 km/h**	
2. Reutemann	Williams-Ford	77	1:32:23.347	
3. Arnoux	Renault	77	1:32:36.301	
4. Lauda	McLaren-Ford	77	1:32:40.514	
5. Rosberg	Williams-Ford	77	1:32:54.540	
6. Watson	McLaren-Ford	77	1:32:59.394	
7. Alboreto	Tyrrell-Ford	76	1 lap	
8. De Angelis	Lotus-Ford	76	1 lap	
9. Salazar	ATS-Ford	75	2 laps	
10. Winkelhock	ATS-Ford	75	2 laps	
11. Giacomelli	Alfa Romeo	74	3 laps	
12. Mass	March-Ford	74	3 laps	
13. De Cesaris	Alfa Romeo	74	3 laps	
14. Daly	Theodore-Ford	73	4 laps	
15. Boesel	March-Ford	72	5 laps	
16. Borgudd	Tyrrell-Ford	72	5 laps	
17. Serra	Fittipaldi-Ford	72	5 laps	
18. Pironi	Ferrari	71	Engine	

RETIREMENTS

Laffite	Ligier-Matra	54	Engine misfire
Warwick	Toleman-Hart	44	Accident
Patrese	Brabham-BMW	18	Turbo/oil problem
Cheever	Ligier-Matra	11	Ignition
Villeneuve	Ferrari	6	Turbo
Piquet	Brabham-BMW	3	Accident
Mansell	Lotus-Ford	0	Electrics/accident
Jarier	Osella-Ford	0	Accident

FASTEST RACE LAP

Prost Renault		1:08.278 216.386 km/h

_PROST'S PERFORMANCE IN THE SOUTH AFRICAN GRAND PRIX

YEAR	CIRCUIT	QUALIFYING	POSITION IN RACE	CAR
1980	Kyalami	22nd	Scratched (accident in qualifying)	McLaren-Ford
1982	Kyalami	5th	**1st**	Renault
1983	Kyalami	5th	Retired (turbo)	Renault
1984	Kyalami	5th	2nd	McLaren-TAG Porsche
1985	Kyalami	9th	3rd	McLaren-TAG Porsche
1993	New Kyalami	**Pole Position**	**1st**	Williams-Renault

73

Chapter **10**
1983
The big disappointment

• **55**_After the trials and tribulations of 1982 and the messed up start to this season, Prost needed to win as soon as possible to get back on course. At Paul Ricard, he was dominant from start to finish!

Sunday, 17th April 1983, Paul Ricard circuit. On the topmost step of the podium, Alain Prost smiles and raises his arms. He has just taken his second French Grand Prix victory and his first win of the year. It was reassuring for him and the entire team. Caught short by a late change in the rules that saw skirts disappear at the end of 1982, Renault-Sport did not have enough time to get the new RE40 ready in time for the opening race of the season in Brazil just two minutes later. Thinking that their rivals would be in the same boat, the French team had turned up in Rio with only intermediate cars, which were no good at all. In the Brabham camp, Gordon Murray had forged ahead, building the BT52 in record time and thanks to his efforts, Nelson Piquet won the first race. Trying to react with alacrity, Renault brought an RE40 to Long Beach, but with insufficient preparation time, Alain could do no better than fight his way round for a 12th place finish. There was a month and a half between the American and French events and Renault therefore had time to fine tune the

RE40 without panicking. The results were impressive as Prost and Cheever monopolised the front row, with the Frenchman sticking it to his team-mate to the tune of 2 seconds! The win came just as easily and after the third round of the 1983 championship, Alain Prost was only 6 points down on the leader, Nelson Piquet.

Having got the measure of his car and his rivals, the Frenchman then displayed impressive consistency all the way to the Austrian Grand Prix, with the exception of the United States and Canadian Grands Prix. Not only did he manage his races intelligently, going for points when a win was not on the cards, but he also showed panache on his way to four victories in France, Belgium, Great Britain and Austria, which put him comfortably in the lead of the championship. It was on the brand new track layout at Spa-Francorchamps that Prost really made the break from the pack. On top of that, winning on a track that required finesse and courage sealed his glorious reputation. At Silverstone, his rivals had to watch powerless as the "professor" did his

1983
Renault RE30C

Same technical caracteristics then RE30B, except:

Engine EF1 Monaco

Transmission
Gearbox/Number of gears: Renault/Hewland (5)
Clutch: Borg&Beck

Dimensions
Track: 1740 mm (Front) / 1630 mm (Rear)
Dry weight: 580 kg

Raced in Brazil.

Designer: Renault Sport Design Team

Engine

Make/Type: Renault EF1 Monaco
Number of Cylinders/Configuration: V6 (Rear)
Capacity: 1492 cc
Bore/Stroke: 86 x 42.8 mm
Compression ratio: 7:1
Turbo(s): 2, KKK
Maximum power: 650 hp
Maximum revs: 12000 rpm
Block material: Aluminium
Fuel/Oil: Elf
Sparking plugs: Champion
Injection: Kugelfischer électronique
Valve gear: 4 ACT
Number of valves per cylinder: 4
Ignition: Marelli
Weight (without intercoolers): 170 kg

Transmission

Weight (without intercoolers): Renault/Hewland (5)
Clutch: Borg&Beck

Chassis

Type: Aluminium monocoque
Suspension: Upper wishbones with pullrods, Front and Rear springs
Shock absorbers: De Carbon
Rim diameter: 13" (Front and Rear)
Rim width: 11.5" (Front) / 16.5" (Rear)
Tyres: Michelin
Brakes: Lockheed

Dimensions

Wheelbase: 2730 mm
Track: 1740 mm (Front) / 1630 mm (Rear)
Dry weight: 543 kg
Fuel capacity: 250 litres

Raced from Long Beach (United States West) to South Africa.

stuff. He had a good look at the Goodyears on Arnoux and Tambay's Ferraris and then forced them to ruin their tyres in the opening laps by pushing very hard. Overtaking them then became child's play. Finally, in Austria, he silenced his detractors who claimed he was too much of a "points shopper," by watching them scrap at a distance, before moving in for the kill when he reckoned they had shot their bolt. After the Austrian Grand Prix, Alain Prost had 51 points, with Piquet on 37 and Arnoux on 34 the only other men still in with a chance of the title. There were only four races to go and everyone was predicting that Prost and Renault would be crowned champions come the end of the season. It was from this point on that everything began to go wrong.

As he tried to pass race leader Piquet in the Dutch Grand Prix, Prost lost control of his car and both the Renault and Brabham were knocked out. One could be forgiven for thinking the incident worked in the Frenchman's favour as there were now just three races to go. However, Prost now had plenty to worry about! He had serious doubts about the performance of the BMW engine that powered the Brabham. The German four cylinder seemed to have found some extra horsepower from somewhere, but the question was where? Elf suspected a "special" fuel and Alain alerted the Renault team to the problem. But relations were going from bad to worse between the team and its star driver and the tension was palpable in the French clan as the year drew to a close. Added to these problems was the fact the

• **56**_On the recently revised, reworked and spectacular Spa-Francorchamps circuit, it was an unexpected Andrea de Cesaris who led in his Alfa Romeo ahead of Prost and Tambay. Unfortunately for the whimsical Italian, his engine gave up in the middle of the race and Alain, who hardly let this display unsettle him, cruised calmly to a welcome win.

technical crew was having great difficulty in improving the V6 that was already running in the red. It was pushing Alain to think of leaving Renault come the end of the year. He got in touch with Ferrari, but he was strongly advised against continuing negotiations with the Scuderia by François Guiter. *"I told him he was mad. He was on the way to winning the world championship and he was planning to tell his team he was leaving at the end of the year. It would completely screw up his chances!"* Prost therefore kept his escape plan under wraps to maintain his title hopes, but no one in the team was fooled. One way or another, a decision would have to be taken come the end of the year.

Upset by the current situation, mortified by the criticism of his failed duel with Piquet and agonising over the technical stagnation at Renault, Alain was clearly weakened

psychologically as he went into the final round with the whole of France hoping it would end in a magnificent victory. Renault even launched a poster campaign urging the public to support its driver. But the public had no inkling that a wheel had fallen off the Renault-Sport wagon. In Monza, Alain did not seem at ease and was nervous and sullen. A broken turbo in the race would send him into a spiral of doubt, especially as Piquet scored a convincing victory. A fortnight later, the Brazilian did it again at Brands Hatch while the Frenchman saved his bacon with a welcome second place. He now had a slender two point lead over his rival and the showdown would take place in the rarified altitude of Kyalami. *"We knew that because of the altitude at Kyalami, we had every chance of breaking and we did,"* Prost recalls today. There was a marked contrast between the grim mood that gripped the

● **57**_With a fourth win at the superb Osterreichring, everyone thought Alain Prost had made the break in the championship from his rival Piquet. But the Frenchman knew the end of the season would be tough.

● **58**_The collision that used up a lot of ink. No matter that Prost claimed he had to get past Piquet as soon as possible because Arnoux was catching them, his optimistic move was criticised by the majority of pundits. For his part, Nelson was not angry with his mate Alain and the two men even dined together later that evening.

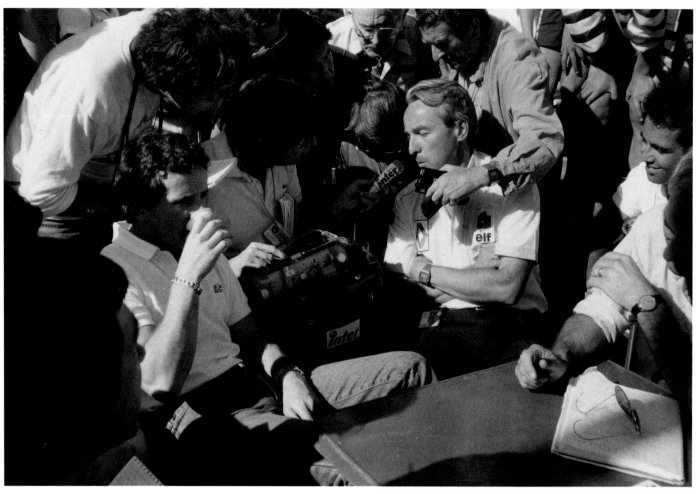

• **59**_At the end of the season, the atmosphere in the Renault camp was tense and miserable. Prost no longer trusted in his team which he accused of not taking his warnings seriously as to the sudden power advantage of the BMW powered Brabhams. Gérard Larrousse tries to smooth things over for the press.

• **60**_In Kyalami, a nervous and anxious Prost tries to force a laugh at Piquet's jokes. The cheeky Brazilian had put this sticker on the Renault, but Alain removed it and stuck it on his overalls, which seemed to amuse Nelson's girlfriend, Sylvia.

Renault pits at the South African circuit and the relaxed atmosphere in the Brabham camp. Piquet even found time to stroll over and mess about with Alain for the benefit of the cameras. Despite their fight, the two men got on well and Nelson had invited Alain to spend time relaxing on his yacht in Monaco harbour. Prost forced a smile, but his heart was not in it. . Qualifying again showed up the Renault engine's lack of punch compared with the BMW and the race would reveal the weaknesses of the French V6. On lap 35, a turbo let go, forcing the inevitable retirement. Determined to play the game to the bitter end, Prost stayed on the pit wall to watch the Brabham racing off in the lead, hoping against hope that a failure would allow him to hang onto his advantage and so become champion. But the wily Piquet lifted off at that point, settling for a sage third place that was enough to assure him of the world title. While Nelson was ecstatic on the podium, Alain seemed to be in a big hurry to pack up and leave. *"I had an appointment in two days time with Bernard Hanon (Renault's President,)"* reveals Prost. *"I wasn't mad. I did not think Renault would go so far as to sack me, but the risk was there. That evening, as I took the helicopter at Kyalami, I*

bumped into Marlboro's John Hogan. We spoke for ten minutes and that is how I covered my options standing round the back end of a helicopter."

The epilogue to this chapter in Alain Prost's career will always be a painful one. The great disappointment with which the Kyalami result was met led to a witch hunt and a badly handled imbroglio as to the outcome of the championship. On this last point, Elf had analysed samples of fuel from the Brabham and proved it exceeded the acceptable octane level. It was therefore illegal and Bernie Ecclestone was forced to admit as much a few months later. The fuel supplier therefore pushed Renault to protest in an effort to rescue the lost title. The constructor decided against it, arguing that a title won in the courts a few weeks after the final race would be devalued. Instead they engaged in some very high level discussions with BMW that went over and above purely sporting matters. All the same, twenty years on, all the protagonists in this affair recognise that the lack of action was a grave mistake. As for scapegoats, they were soon selected. On the engine side, Jean-Pierre Boudy fitted the frame and on a far more public front, Alain Prost was singled out. The famous meeting at Renault's head office ended with a divorce "by mutual consent" and it left French fans with a bitter taste to add to their huge disappointment over the lost title. For his part, Alain had his cross to bear, but there was no way he could have realised at the time that the Renault bosses had inadvertently furnished him with an incredible opportunity that would steer his career on the path to untold glories. ■

• **61**_The 1983 South African Grand Prix will always be a wound that refuses to heal for Alain Prost, the Renault team and French race fans. Scores were settled in an underhand way and the only one to eventually emerge unscathed in the short term was Alain.

Chapter 11

1984
The new world

● **63**_Even if it was mainly down to the bad luck of his rivals, Prost's win in the first grand prix of the 1984 season had an important symbolic value. It was the first with his new crew and he laid down a marker for team-mate Lauda.

By the end of 1983, Alain Prost was in need of a breath of fresh air. For over a year, his home life in Saint-Chamond had turned into a nightmare, with anonymous malicious phone calls day and night, his family harassed and two cars torched. He was fed up with these acts prompted by jealousy and sadly stupid human nature. "Socialist France" certainly did not inspire him and he had already considered a move into exile in a more liberal England in 1982. In the end, he chose somewhere nearer to home, in the shape of Switzerland and in April 1983, he fled there to escape the cruelties of his fellow countrymen. Critics immediately latched on to the more agreeable fiscal climate to be found in his new home. *"Nobody believes me when I say it, but it really was 80% for the quality of life and 20% for the tax benefits. You have to remember that in karting, Formula Renault and in F3, no one earned any money. Tackling my fourth season of F1, I sold up everything and left with just 300,000 francs in my pocket! So, finances didn't really come into it. If that had been the main reason I would have done better moving to England where the situation would have been even more favourable on that score."* At the time, Swiss law regarding the status of residents meant

that Alain could not buy property and had to settle for renting an apartment at first. But at least it brought physical stability and to that was added a mental reconstitution.

Marlboro was determined to do all in its power to find a good berth for its favourite son, who had been kicked out of his team. The annoying thing was that at this time of year, theoretically all the seats were taken. But then came a stroke of luck: Ron Dennis was not immune to the plight of little Alain, whom he'd had to regretfully let go at the end of 1980 when he took over the reins of the McLaren team. His driver line-up was complete with Niki Lauda and John Watson, but the Irishman was delaying signing his contract as he tried to extract a better financial deal before putting pen to paper. Dennis was not that keen on an ageing Watson when he could imagine slotting the young and ambitious Prost alongside the experienced and wily Niki Lauda to create the dream team. Alain's meeting with Dennis was brokered by Marlboro and it did not take long for him to agree terms with the Englishman. It was not as though he was spoilt for choice and Ron's offer was mouth-watering anyway. He would get to drive alongside Niki Lauda in a revolutionary car, built entirely in

Designer: John Barnard

Engine

Make/Type: TAG-Porsche P01 (TTE P01)
Number of Cylinders/Configuration: V6 (Rear)
Capacity: 1489 cc
Bore/Stroke: 82 x 47 mm
Compression ratio: 7.5 :1
Turbo(s): 2, KKK
Maximum power: 750 hp
Maximum revs: 11500 rpm
Block material: Alliage Aluminium
Fuel/Oil: Shell
Sparking plugs: Unipart
Injection: Bosch Motronic MS3
Valve gear: 4 ACT
Number of valves per cylinder: 4
Ignition: Bosch Motronic MS3
Weight: 145 kg (without turbos, intercoolers or exhausts)

Transmission

Gearbox/Number of gears: McLaren Hewland (5)
Clutch: AP/Borg&Beck

Chassis

Type: Carbon monocoque
Suspension: Auxilliary rockers, lower wishbone with springs at Front; rockers, lower wishbone with springs at Rear.
Shock absorbers: Bilstein
Rim diameter: 13" (Front and Rear)
Rim width: 11.75" (Front) / 16.25" (Rear)
Tyres: Michelin
Brakes: McLaren/SEP

Dimensions

Wheelbase: 2 794 mm
Track: 1816 mm (Front) / 1676 mm (Rear)
Dry weight: 540 kg
Fuel capacity: 220 litres

Used all season.

carbon fibre and powered by a Porsche V6 paid for by the powerful Saudi TAG group. As for a salary, Prost obviously did not have a leg to stand on when it came to negotiating a deal. *"I wasn't unhappy,"* insists Alain. *"In any case, the contract was better than what I was getting at Renault and I also got a bonus per point and for wins. All in all, I didn't do too badly on the deal."* Alain Prost had just discovered a new world, as John Watson left by the back door.

Working alongside Niki Lauda had a special significance for the young Frenchman. When he was charging off ahead of the chasing pack in karting in 1975, Niki Lauda and his splendid Ferrari 312 T was doing the same in Formula 1. Prost the kid had pinned photos of his hero on his bedroom wall! *"Niki was one of my childhood idols. I finally got to meet him at Kyalami in 1982. But this time round, he was not the authoritative figure he used to be and one had the impression that he was taking something of*

a back seat, like a rookie just arriving in the paddock. Actually, everyone thought he had only come back for the money and we were all waiting to see what would happen. And boy did we see! It didn't look like it, but he was serious and on the pace." Lauda had come back to work to help Dennis get the Porsche engine, sort out the new car and then start winning. The famous MP4-2 TAG Porsche designed by John Barnard had made its debut in September 1983 at the Dutch Grand Prix, the race where Alain began his downward spiral. It meant that by this time, Niki had smoothed out all its rough edges when Alain got behind the wheel for the first test of the 83-84 winter at the Paul Ricard circuit. The Frenchman was delighted with his first impressions. The car seemed fantastic and he was very pleased to find an almost unchanged team. *"All the good elements from 1980 had stayed put. The atmosphere was fun and a complete contrast to the heavy scene I had lived through*

• **64**_In apocalyptic conditions, Alain Prost showed himself to be the best sailor in the flooded streets of Monaco. However, a virtually unknown young man, at the wheel of a less than special Toleman-Hart had almost stolen the moment from him. He managed it a few years later.

at Renault." As an attentive pupil, he applied himself to following the advice of Lauda, who distant at first, had soon been reassured by the good intentions of his young *team-mate*. Alain really intended to form a tight knit unit with Niki and all the McLaren crew. But naturally it did not stop him from beating the Austrian as soon as the chance arose.

McLaren enjoyed an exceptional 1984 season, beating a pile of Formula 1 records. The Lauda-Prost driver pairing turned out to be alarmingly efficient and destroyed any hope of resistance from the opposition who were dealt a knockout blow right from the start. The game ended up being played out between these two stars and ended in the apotheosis of suspense, the like of which has never been seen since. Formula 1 has seen its share of gripping duels, but few had been as fascinating and that was down to the personalities of the protagonists. Alain Prost perfectly complemented his alter-ego and it is true to say that this first year with McLaren marked the real end of his apprenticeship.

For the first time in his career, he came up against someone who could teach him a thing or

two when it came to setting up a car. Above and beyond that, Alain learnt a great deal about managing a race as well as developing an understanding of his own attitude. Professor Lauda was remorseless in this respect and the two men soon became inseparable. Lauda taught his young colleague how to avoid wasting time off the track, how to manage his image; in short how to liberate his mind and concentrate it on the coming race. Once school was out, and in between the grand prix weekends, Niki would hijack Alain on long nights of a "liberating" nature which were often hard to recall. *"He was one hell of a party animal and I ended up in one or two memorable drinking sessions,"* recalls Prost with a grin. *"Willy [Dungl, Lauda's trainer] would say to us: "Sunday night, go and let your hair down! But Monday morning, it ends!" I remember a session in Vienna that went on all night. We were supposed to attend a motor show and we never got to bed. When the show opened at eight in the morning, we were completely out of it. Mind you, three glasses are enough for me! Niki had a shower cap on his head, if you can imagine that. We had to make a short speech and it was all a bit of an effort,"* he recalls with a smile...

Niki Lauda: "Beating Prost became a challenge for me"

A double world champion in 1975 and 1977 with Ferrari, Niki Lauda quit Formula 1 in 1979, making a comeback in 1982 to answer the call from Ron Dennis. In 1984, he came up against his sternest rival:

"Alain's arrival at McLaren was a total surprise for me, because right up to the last minute he was a Renault driver. It was okay for me, just another team-mate. The only problem was that he was quicker than me and he bore no comparison to John Watson!

At first, I was not so impressed because I had more experience than him when it came to the races. But he improved bit by bit and then life got a bit more difficult. I had to further perfect my driving style and beating him became a challenge for me. I quickly realised that I couldn't in qualifying and so I changed my race strategy. I concentrated on getting my car set up as well as possible, using all my experience. You know, we came from different generations. When he was learning to drive, I was already world champion with Ferrari. And I passed on as much of my experience as I could. He was also a quick learner when it came to the pleasures in life and because of that, we got on famously."

Right from the start of the championship, Alain turned out to be quicker than Niki in all aspects of the art, from qualifying to the race. He took an incredibly short time to adapt to this new world and he immediately proved to be a formidable opponent for the Austrian champion who soon realised he might have bitten off more than he could chew. At the wheel of the very quick MP4-2, the Frenchman worked miracles. Apart from his wins in the first half of the season in Brazil, San Marino and Monaco, his evident brio and command of the subject saw him get out of apparently hopeless situations. In South Africa, he was forced to start dead last from the pits at the wheel of the spare car that had been set up for Lauda. He then set about charging through the field at a breathtaking rate, just as he had done in '82, to end up in an unexpected second place behind his team leader. At Imola, he was leading before a spin, when he was caught out by a faulty brake master cylinder. Even though he was flat out at the time, he stayed in control of the McLaren as it went through 360 degrees, before carrying on to take one of his best wins. Luck rather than skill intervened in Rio, when Lauda then Derek Warwick dropped out while leading. In Monaco he was the winner when the chequered flag was shown before half distance in confusing circumstances. He was in trouble with his brakes at the time in torrential rain and he was saved by the race being stopped, much to the despair of the man who was about to overtake him: a young rookie by the name of Ayrton Senna. Luck

abandoned him on the North American leg which had never inspired him much.

From then on, he was equally remarkable, even quicker and more determined, taking four more comfortable wins. He thus equalled Jim Clark's famous record for seven wins in a season in 1963, although it has to be said that Clark did it in just 10 races, compared to 16 for Prost. The Frenchman was now considered to be one of the best drivers in the world. But not the best. In 1984, this title went to the wily Niki Lauda by....half a point! The Austrian had shown exemplary consistency in the last seven races, picking up three wins, three seconds and a fourth. Alain alternated wins in Germany, Holland, Europe and Portugal with retirements. He was leading in England and knew his team-mate was closing so he picked up the pace and showed a rare aggression that did not go down well with the McLaren gearbox. In Austria, he had to steer one handed while holding a recalcitrant gear lever in gear, before spinning off on a patch of oil. Finally, in Italy, his engine blew up after just three laps! Essentially, a bit of bad luck and a bit too much of a hurry saw him miss out on important points which would have easily been enough for him to reach his long awaited goal, given the tiny gap that separated him from Lauda. However, as the final round approached, there was still everything to play for.

At the start of the Portuguese Grand Prix at Estoril, Alain led by 3.5 points, the untidy half point came courtesy of Monaco where he won

• 66_By winning the 1984 Dutch Grand Prix, Prost, seen here lapping Tambay (no. 15) and de Angelis (no. 11,) propelled McLaren into the record books. It was the first time a team had won nine races in a season. The previous record dated back to 1978 when Lotus took eight wins. In 1984, McLaren would extend the record to twelve!

• 67_In a class of his own, but it was not enough! Against the typically Mediterranean backdrop of the Estoril circuit, Alain Prost was leading as he pleased, with no control over what was going on behind. Unfortunately, that was where the title was decided in this last race!

• **68**_Plenty of emotion on the Estoril podium. Niki Lauda had pulled off an incredible gamble to take the world championship again after a gap of two years. Alain Prost had lost by the smallest of margins and was fighting back the tears, while Ron Dennis savoured his dream team's crushing domination this season. As for Ayrton Senna, he was convinced he would soon be fighting for the title.

with 4.5 points awarded for a race shortened to less than three quarters distance. The sums were easy. He had to win, with Lauda doing no better than third. It looked entirely feasible as the Austrian had only qualified eleventh while Prost was on the front row alongside Piquet. In theory, it was an obvious advantage, but in practice things did not work out that way. The McLarens were so superior to the other cars that Niki found it relatively straightforward to pick

his way through the field. Meanwhile, Alain was comfortably in the lead, but he now realised that the outcome of the championship was no longer in his hands. For twenty laps, he was told that Lauda was only third. Comfortably ensconced in second place, Nigel Mansell in the Lotus was his last line of defence. On lap 52, McLaren hung out Prost's pit board with the message, "Lauda –2." The Lotus had lost its brakes. Prost then had to dig deep within his reserves of motivation and self-belief to win the grand prix. He had done all that could have been asked of him. He had been the best driver that year, but Lauda had known how to be the most consistent and triumphed by the skin of his teeth and the most miniscule points difference in the history of Formula 1!

On the top step of the podium, Alain kept it all together and, in a sporting gesture, pulled his team-mate up with him to take the long applause of the crowd. He listened to Niki's words of comfort, knowing that next year would be his. It freed him to savour the enjoyment of the exceptional battle they had just staged for the crowd and for spectators the world over. The party went on long into the night and an endless round of celebrations organised by Marlboro over the next few days served to cement a feeling of immense mutual respect between Alain Prost and Niki Lauda. Those who, for want of anything better to do, expected them to be at loggerheads were to be disappointed! ∎

Chapter 12
1985
A place in history

• **70**_In 1985, Alain Prost's name appeared on the Monaco Grand Prix winner's trophy for the second consecutive year. Michele Alboreto had been quicker that day, but impetuosity got the better of him and he lost some places, while the "Professor" dealt with a malfunctioning engine perfectly, at the same time hiding the fault from the opposition. A truly great strategic win.

At the end of his fifth season in Formula 1, Alain Prost finally set off for a real family holiday in San Domingo. The year-long battle had marked him and he was running on empty. A few days spent as a family man recharged his batteries in preparation for what he expected to be a year full of potential pitfalls. Twice he had been the favourite and twice he had been pipped at the post. Alain was superstitious, but more than that he was the sort to hang on tight. As long as he was given the means, he would not budge an inch in pursuit of his goals. He displayed these characteristics throughout his career and failure was never part of his vocabulary. His ambition had increased tenfold and he made that clear to Ron Dennis when he signed his new contract and the McLaren boss played fair and acceded to the financial demands, which were not excessive given that he was dealing with one of the best drivers of his generation. This new status allowed Alain to finally achieve his childhood dream of buying his own house. He had an old farm rebuilt in the quiet village of Yens, near Geneva. The country life near a large city was all the little chap aspired to now he was rich and famous. Now, just the most important element was missing. On the eve of the 1985 season, Prost was chewing his nails even more than ever. The new MP4-2B would not be

ready until just before it was time to head for Brazil. It was typical of Barnard the perfectionist who liked to tinker with his latest creations until the very last moment. Lauda did not seem that motivated and Alain logically expected the McLaren troops to rest on their laurels after their 1984 triumph. Added to this was the opposition, starved of success and keen to wash away the humiliation of the previous year. The Frenchman thought that the road to the top would once again be damned steep. As he stepped out of the cockpit in Rio, he could smile and relax completely. He had just won the grand prix, even lifting off towards the end, winning as he pleased. The MP4-2B was reliable and rapid. But it was not the quickest as the Ferraris, Williams and Lotus seemed to have made enormous progress. The following grand prix, run at Estoril in the pouring rain, would shuffle the cards in the hierarchy pack, but more than that it was the race where Ayrton Senna's talent was finally plain for all to see. For Alain, it was a race to forget. He was caught out by a dose of aquaplaning and spun off down the main straight and hit the barriers. Behind Senna, Alboreto and his Ferrari picked up a welcome second place to add to the one he scored in Brazil. He thus led the championship while Alain was second equal with the new Brazilian phenomenon. He therefore left Portugal

with a pretty clear idea of what he was up against this year. For his part, Niki Lauda had suffered a second retirement, but seemed not a bit bothered by it all.

After a staggering run of mechanical failures, Ayrton Senna soon disappeared from Prost's sights, while Michele Alboreto turned out to be a more formidable foe. He and Alain were quite close in qualifying, usually beaten by the fragile missiles of Senna and Rosberg. In the Porsche camp, reliability in the race was the main weapon rather than getting caught up in a meaningless qualifying contest. In 1985, the

disposable qualifying engine was all the rage, designed to last for just two or three laps while putting out a mind-blowing 1000 horsepower or more! Alain preferred to concentrate on his race set-up which explains why his name rarely appeared at the top of the time sheet, but would be seen more often heading the more important race result. That's what happened at Imola where he triumphed over the speed freaks and those who ran out fuel. But he did not triumph over the stewards, who disqualified him after his car was found to be 2kg underweight. He made up for it by winning at Monaco to go equal on points with Alboreto.

• **71**_Alain takes the chequered flag to win at Silverstone but remains stoic about it. The flag waver had got it wrong by one lap and having been warned from the pits, the Frenchman prudently did an extra lap before showing his delight.

Designer: John Barnard

Same technical caracteristics then MP4/2 except:

Engine
Maximum revs: 12000 rpm
Maximum power: 800 hp
Injection and ignition: Bosch Motronic MP14

Transmission
Gearbox/Number of gears: McLaren (5)
Clutch: AP

Chassis
Tyres: Goodyear

Dimensions
Wheelbase: 2692 mm
Track: 1835 mm (Front) / 1683 mm(Rear)
Dry weight: 540 kg
Fuel capacity: 220 litres

Used all season.

• **72**_Alain and Michele fought tooth and nail but shared a mutual respect. The two men really got on and never missed an opportunity to show it.

The 1985 championship was proving something of a paradox for Alain, given that he showed a total mastery of his car and was able to display his immense ability as a driver and yet he was forced to chase after Michele in the title race! At the end of the North American campaign, the Italian had extended the gap still further. However, as he was well aware, the hare does not always beat the tortoise! Prost's optimism remained indestructible, as he felt the summer circuits would provide more propitious conditions for his car to show its full potential. And that is exactly what happened. It was a close contest between the two men at the top of the table in the run up to the Austrian Grand Prix where they ended up equal on points with 50 each, although Prost had the more sparkling record, out shining Alboreto by four wins to two. In Holland, Alain finished ahead of Michele but behind Lauda. The Austrian had announced he would be retiring at the end of the season and he was keen to add one more win to his records and thus turned up the wick a bit on the turbo. Prost raised this matter with him after the race, but Niki reassured him that he would help him when the time came, even if he was sure that there would be no need of assistance for Alain to be champion. In the end, Prost had absolutely no need of Lauda's help to take the honours.

Starting with the Italian Grand Prix, the Ferrari V6 engine consistently refused to let Michele see the chequered flag. In Monza, Alain Prost had in any case beaten his rival well before the turbo exploded on the Italian car. As the Honda in Keke Rosberg's Williams also gave up the ghost, Alain was able to cruise to a fifth win of the season. In Spa, he was magnificent in qualifying, but it rained for the race and Alain remembered Estoril and thought of the championship. He therefore did not attempt to counter the flying Ayrton Senna and finished a comfortable third. The hour of coronation was approaching.

It happened on English soil at Brands Hatch, back then one of the temples of British motor sport. Prost drove a totally calculating race to the fourth place he needed. The connoisseur English fans appreciated his performance and gave him a well deserved ovation when he was called up onto the podium. Nigel Mansell, who took his first grand prix win that day, made plenty of room on the top step for the first ever Frenchman to become Formula 1 Drivers' World Champion. Alain Prost had now joined the world motor sport elite as well as becoming a legend in the pantheon of French sport. From this point on, his name could be mentioned in the same breath as Jean-Claude

● **73**_One cannot claim that Alain Prost gave a masterly display at the wheel at Brands Hatch on 6 October 1985, but it was a tactical performance from a man who had previously paid dearly for losing two championships by a gnat's whisker and who this time had decided to do whatever it took to be crowned champion. He did what was needed with a steady fourth place.

BORDEAUX SE REBIFFE NANTES SE CONCENTRE

Girondins et Nantais n'ont pas laissé Paris-SG prendre un peu plus le large, et sont toujours à six points du leader. Les champions sortants, retrouvant solidité et efficacité, ont remporté une probante victoire à Toulouse (2-1). Et les Jaunes se sont débarrassés sans douleur de Nancy (2-0), avant de venir affronter l'ogre parisien dans son antre du Parc, vendredi soir.

(Pages 2 et 3)

Noah, Leconte plus dure est la chute

Battue par la Yougoslavie, la France jouera l'an prochain en Deuxième Division. Samedi, la victoire du double avait reculé l'échéance ; mais hier, Noah n'a rien pu faire contre Zivojinovic. En 1982, la France disputait la finale de la Coupe Davis. Cette année, ce seront l'Allemagne et la Suède.

(Page 18)

LUNDI 7 OCTOBRE 1985

5,50 F

40° ANNÉE - N° 12 258

L'ÉQUIPE

LE QUOTIDIEN DU SPORT ET DE L'AUTOMOBILE

IL PASSE A LA PROSTERITE

Alain Prost est champion du monde de Formule I. Il est le premier Français à remporter ce titre, dans une compétition qui existe depuis 1950. Hier à Brands Hatch, où Mansell a gagné le premier Grand Prix de sa carrière, Prost (4e) a pris les trois points qui le mettent à l'abri d'un éventuel retour d'Alboreto dans les prochains Grands Prix.

(Pages 20 à 22)

(Photo Patrick BOUTROUX)

Hors série SPECIAL F 1

En vente mercredi 9 F

CYCLISME

LUDO PEETERS COMME EN 1983

Ludo Peeters est l'homme de l'automne. Comme en 1983, il s'est imposé dans Créteil-Chaville avec quelques secondes d'avance sur un petit groupe de six hommes qu'il avait surpris à 6 kilomètres de l'arrivée. Kelly et Argentin, qui faisaient figure de grands favoris, se firent surprendre par le métier du Belge.

(Pages 14 et 15)

VOLLEY BALL

DU BRONZE... EN ATTENDANT MIEUX

Victoire sur l'Italie, défaite devant l'URSS. Rien de bien étonnant pour ces deux derniers matches des Championnats d'Europe. A l'arrivée, une troisième place et une médaille de bronze pour l'équipe de France. Une éclatante confirmation du sérieux travail accompli depuis quelques mois en vue du Championnat du monde 1986 en France.

(Page 6)

Jurkovitz, Devos et Faure, un contre efficace.

BASKET

LIMOGES RETROUVÉ

Avec un Knight en verve (54 points), Limoges a fait oublier son petit début de saison. Un succès (126-94) devant le Stade Français qui rassure. Les deux leaders continuent sur leur lancée : victoire de Villeurbanne à Challans (106-103), succès de Monaco sur Le Mans (95-88).

(Page 10)

GOLF

LANCÔME : PRICE EN PLAY-OFF

Nick Price et Mark James se sont livré un magnifique coude à coude au 16° Trophée Lancôme. Et ils durent aller jusqu'à un play-off pour se départager. Le Sud-Africain Price l'emporta finalement au soixante-quinzième trou. Excellent résultat pour Emmanuel Dussart, qui termine seizième pour sa première participation au Lancôme.

(Page 13)

RUGBY

COUP DE TABAC SUR TOULON

Quatrième victoire d'affilée pour le Stade Toulousain, pour Agen et pour Tarbes, vainqueurs respectifs de Narbonne (13-15), du Creusot (22-15) et du Racing (26-12). C'est la première défaite des Parisiens, ainsi que de Toulon, battu à Valence (13-22) par la botte de l'ouvreur tahitien Richard Mapuhi, auteur de 15 points.

(Pages 16 et 17)

ET AUSSI...

Bateaux p. 19	Haltérophilie p. 19	Moto p. 19
Boxe p. 18	Handball p. 19	Natation p. 10
Canoë-kayak p. 15	Hippisme p. 18	Tennis de table p. 6
Équitation p. 19	Hockey p. 18	Tir à l'arc p. 6
Glace p. 6	Jeu à XIII p. 11	Tous les sports p. 6

LOTO SPORTIF L'EQUIPE VOUS EN DIT PLUS !

On connaîtra ce soir le nombre des gagnants et les gains du septième tirage du Loto sportif. Compte tenu des surprises et de l'augmentation (+ 50 %) de la recette, ces derniers devraient être importants. Mais, déjà, ce sont les prochains pronostics qui retiennent l'attention. Dès aujourd'hui, L'Equipe vous présente la nouvelle grille, avec en vedette P-SG - Nantes, une des têtes du Championnat de Première Division. Tous les jours, vous trouverez dans nos colonnes des informations pour vous aider à gagner. Et mercredi, trois pages spéciales avec le tableau analytique, les conseils de Roger Piantoni et la synthèse des spécialistes de L'Equipe.

(Page 6)

MARITA KOCH : L'EXPLOIT !

En reprenant le record du monde du 400 m et en l'abaissant à 47''60 (notre photo), Marita Koch a réalisé un exploit prodigieux. Elle a emmené la RDA vers le succès dans la Coupe du monde, alors que les Etats-Unis s'imposaient chez les hommes.

(Page 11)

(Téléphoto REUTER)

Chefs d'entreprises, comme vous 1 078 000 cadres lisent l'Equipe Chaque lundi matin. (Les jobs de « L'Equipe Carrières », pages 12 et 13)

L'Equipe, le seul vrai quotidien national pour offrir ou trouver un emploi.

Killy, Yannick Noah, Michel Platini, Bernard Hinault and all those who had held high their national colours. However, during the endless interviews and media appearance he was called on to make, Alain never looked quite as delighted as one might have expected. *"Naturally, I was proud to be the first Frenchman to be world champion. But there had been so much criticism beforehand, there had been so much talk that I would never be champion that it led to me holding back somewhat. I would have liked to have been champion with Renault but instead I spent all my time with Ron, Mansour, the McLaren team, the English basically and I was almost a bit embarrassed by that. It's my chauvinist side coming out."* The real fans were simply delighted that finally a driver had shown his country how to win. And he deserved the plaudits for his meteoric rise built on a full armoury of driving talents, a mix of brio, sensitivity and anticipation. ■

John Barnard:
"Sometimes I felt like kicking him out"

The designer of the MP4-1, built entirely from carbon fibre, John Barnard was McLaren technical director from 1980 to 1986. Here he gives us his assessment of Alain Prost:

"He could spend hours talking to me. The good side was that by talking a lot, you gather a lot of information and detail. But in the end, you get saturated and you had to tell him it was time to make a decision. In fact what you want to say to him is: "Okay Alain, now go away and find something else to do (laughs.) He had an incredible thirst for knowledge so that he could work even more on his car to get the absolute maximum out of it. His technical feedback was fantastic and we had an excellent working relationship. He was very kind to his equipment. Alain's great strength, which I never encountered again with any other driver, was his ability to get through the turns and corners with what most other drivers would consider a huge amount of understeer. But the way Alain drove there was no understeer. The classic example was Rosberg. He wanted a car that would allow him to brake at the very last moment as deep as possible into the corner, before chucking the car as though it was a kart. To do that, he had a huge amount of downforce on the front of the car. But that made the car very hard to balance, you lost traction at the rear and therefore you lost time. With his driving style, Alain only needed minimal downforce at the front, with soft suspension and only very little anti-roll bar. And the way he placed his car in the corner meant he never had understeer. And I don't think there were many other drivers who understood how to do that. Niki was quite close to Alain on this score, but he was not on the same level."

• **76**_A rare privilege: in the spring of 1986, the airforce gave the new world champion his first ever flight in a Mirage so that he could experience the mind blowing acceleration of the jet. Having loved it, Alain was pleased to go for a second flight a few years later when he took his fourth title.

Chapter 13
1986-1987
Chasing the records

Having won the world title, Alain Prost was now part of what might be regarded as a sporting superstar elite. But while he took advantage of the material gains, he kept a cool head. Pragmatism and humble origins kept him grounded. He only touched a small amount of his now sizeable wealth and invested the rest. The driver had evolved into a canny businessman with a knack for managing his image in a very professional manner. His main priority was the well being of his nearest and dearest and he did not fritter his money away on the trappings of luxury so beloved of many stars. He did not own a yacht nor a Lear jet and did not throw his cash around. He was happy with his beautiful house which had at last been finished. He drove a comfortable saloon car: *"it's very quiet and automatic,"* but was not into extravagant means of transport. For long journeys he chartered a private plane. Alain now had a very comfortable life but it was not extravagant, in stark contrast to that of his new team-mate, Keke Rosberg.

World Champion with Williams in 1982, the Finn with his Californian rock star image was a flamboyant character both on track and off it. He appreciated the finer things in life and his driving style was amongst the most aggressive and spectacular of all his peers. However, his fighting spirit had captivated Ron Dennis, Mansour Ojjeh and Alain Prost. The Frenchman was now very much at home at McLaren and had a say in whom the team brought in as a team-mate. *"All decisions were taken jointly with Ron and Mansour. I had pushed to get Rosberg, just as I did with Johansson and even with Senna. I always put the interest of the team first."* Keke's abrasive antics at the wheel did not sit easily with the smooth driving style initiated by Lauda and adopted by Prost. Rosberg soon struggled and was generally thrashed by his team-mate, but unlike the usual litany of excuses offered up in these circumstances, the Finn was honest and brave enough to admit to his failings. He later decided to hang up his helmet at the end of 1986, not before giving his prestigious mate a helping hand along the way.

The 1986 season was tough, very tough. Piquet and Mansell and the Williams-Honda soon proved to be the combination to beat and the Japanese engine emerged as the ultimate weapon in the armoury. Far from losing motivation after winning his title, Alain Prost was as sharp as ever and made the most of the slightest mistake from his rivals. He triumphed thanks to those who ran out of fuel in Imola and he crushed his rivals in Monaco on a weekend when he came close to perfection. But from then on, he had to settle for making the most of his McLaren MP4-2C's legendary reliability and its low fuel consumption in light of the new rule restricting fuel capacity to just 195 litres. He picked up the odd precious point behind the irrefutable stars of the summer, Nelson and Nigel. He almost stumbled after a disastrous Hungarian Grand Prix at the brand new Hungaroring in Budapest (where he never won!) and just got back on track in the end by winning in Austria, when his main rivals all retired. It was a tough season on the human side too. Having been enticed away by Scuderia Ferrari, John Barnard, the faithful engineer in whom Alain and Ron Dennis had placed all their trust, left the team during the course of the summer. He was now replaced by one of his assistants, the American, Steve Nichols. On a personal level, Alain found it painful to deal with the death from cancer of his brother Daniel, who had been so in awe of his achievements, a few days before the Portuguese Grand Prix. Ron Dennis and Alain Prost had to face the facts: the Porsche engine had reached the end of its development and the only engine that fitted the bill for an ambitious

team like McLaren was the Honda. Alain was now very much part of the way the team was run and Ron took him with him to Japan in an attempt to try and convince former race mechanic from the Sixties, now company boss, Nobuhiko Kawamoto. *"We signed the contract,"* reveals Alain. *"But Ron was adamant that he wanted to take it home to go over it again. This upset the Japanese and they stayed with Williams for one more year. Personally, I thought it was in the bag when we got home."* Prospects were therefore gloomy as the end of the 1986 season approached and the superiority of the Williams did not help matters. Despite it all, Alain remained confident. He took two great podium finishes in Portugal and Mexico which put him in the running for the title along with Mansell and Piquet in the final round in Adelaide. The Englishman had led the series since the half-season and the Brazilian had moved up to third during the summer. Prost was second. Of the three, only Nigel could settle for a third place finish to be champion, while for Alain and Nelson only a win would do. It was in Australia that Rosberg provided his famous helping hand. In Adelaide, everyone except Alain seemed nervous. He had nothing to lose and everything to gain.

● **79**_In Belgium on a track he liked, Prost had set off intending to win. Berger's impetuous move at the start in his Benetton (no. 20) saw him hit the Frenchman's McLaren and put an end to those plans. Instead of losing hope, Alain drove a brilliant race at the wheel of a chassis that according to John Barnard was "bent like a banana) and climbed back from 23rd place to sixth at the chequered flag. Always an eye on the bigger picture, the "Professor" pointed out that the single point could come in handy at the end of the year.

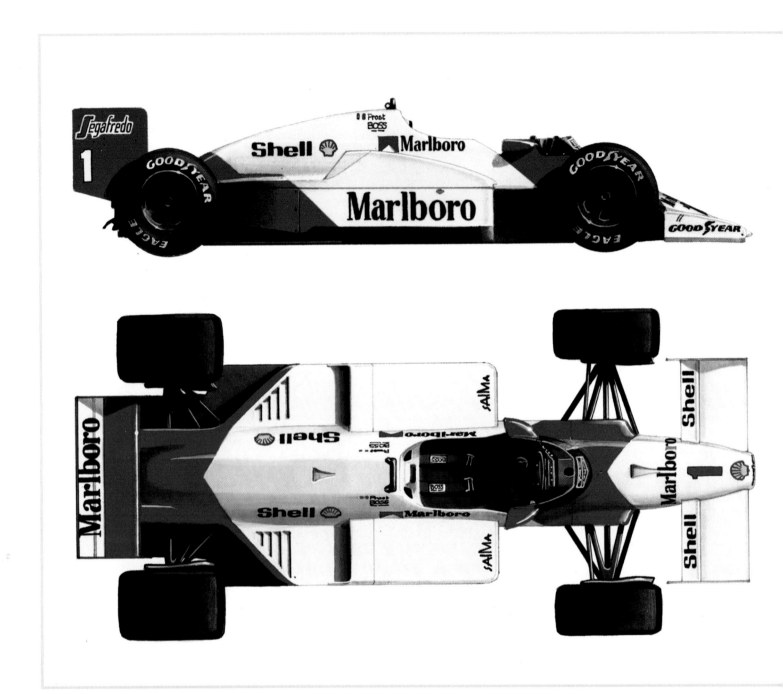

Rosberg made the sort of demon start he was fond of and moved irrevocably into the lead on lap 6. It was his last Formula 1 race and to many it looked like the final cavalry charge of a proud fighter. However, he went along with a carefully thought out plan set out by him and Alain along with the team. Keke was due to run off like a hare to force the Honda drivers to push their tyres too hard. It was planned that Alain would pit at half distance to fit new tyres that would allow him to attack to the maximum. The Finn, would then hand over the lead, partly because he too would have worn out his tyres. Two factors intervened to affect the theoretical strategy and turn this race into a grandiose cliff-hanger.

On lap 32 of 82, Prost headed to the pits with a puncture. *"No one had planned to stop and even Goodyear were unaware of our plans,"* recalls Alain. *"My puncture happened three or four laps before we had intended to stop! Everyone said 'what luck that he had to stop!' But it was the truth as I was due to stop. It was then that we noticed my tyres were hardly worn. But we were aware that there was a risk of high wear or degradation if I had stayed on the same set."* Informed by Goodyear that Alain's tyres were in good condition, Williams decided to leave Piquet and Mansell out on track. It was a mistake. The moustachioed Englishman who was lying third in the championship had a blow out right down the main straight at full speed and Piquet

1986 Australian Grand Prix
McLaren MP4/2C-TAG

Designer: John Barnard

Same technical caracteristics then MP4/2B, except:

Engine
Type: P01
Capacity: 1499 cc
Maximum power: 850 hp

Transmission
Gearbox/Number of gears: McLaren (6)
Clutch: Borg&Beck

Chassis
Wheelbase: 2768 mm
Fuel capacity: 195 litres

Used all season.

was then immediately called into the pits. And who did that leave out in front? The reigning champion, but his calm progress was soon interrupted when the on-board computer clearly showed that at this pace, he would be five litres short of finishing the race! Alain was a pragmatic thinker: if he kept going he would not see the chequered flag. If he lifted off, he would be passed by Piquet who was closing on him. A second place was worthless to him so the rational Prost, the Cartesian Prost set about persuading himself that the computer was on the blink and so he decided to ignore it. Just like that! A few very long laps later, the McLaren no. 1 was first across the finish line to an incredible ovation from the crowd. His arms shot out of the cockpit in a V.

As soon as the red and white car came to a stop, the driver jumped out like a jack in a box and began to leap up and down around his car. On that day, Alain Prost had got the better of his rivals, of bad luck and of state of the art technology. Unflappable in the extreme, the computer read "5 litres."

Winning a world championship is no mean feat, but to take two back to back is rare indeed. Alberto Ascari and Juan Manuel Fangio had managed it in the Fifties, then Jack Brabham did it in 1959 and 1960, but no one else had managed it since. Alain Prost thus entered the record book on 26th October 1986 equalling Jim Clark's record for the greatest number of wins (25) on the way.

● 80_In 1986, the only thing the rule makers could come up with slow the Formula 1 cars was to reduce the size of the fuel cell, which meant a lot of cars ran out of petrol. Prost was caught out like this within metres of the end of the race at Hockenheim, so he jumped out of the cockpit and started pushing the car to the line. It was strictly forbidden, but the Frenchman wanted to put on a public show of disapproval of these new "fuel economy runs."

● 81_In the last round of the 1986 championship, three drivers were still in the running for the title crown: Alain Prost, calm and happy is surrounded by the Williams boys, Nelson Piquet and Nigel Mansell.

That only left Jackie Stewart on 27 out in front, but not for much longer it would seem. Furthermore this second title had been hard to come by at the wheel of a car that was clearly less powerful than the Williams. But the scientific and patient approach of the little Frenchman had made the difference when up against two drivers who kept tripping over one another and playing a solo game. If he had got it wrong in the past in this respect, the "Professor" made up for it in style with this second success that was applauded by his peers, including his mate Piquet, who was the first to congratulate him on the podium. The French public gave him a triumphal welcome a few days later on the Champs-Elysées. Alain Prost was given the exceptional privilege of parading down the famous avenue at the wheel of his faithful MP4-4C, an honour usually reserved for heroes. After all, he had become a sort of hero come the end of 1986.

But the hero knew that a Herculean task faced him on the eve of the 1987 season. The Porsche engine had revealed its limitations in 1986 and there was no sign of any major evolution coming out of Stuttgart, while it was certain that Honda would do all in its power to get a stranglehold on Formula 1. Alain had total confidence in the McLaren engineers, now led

Anne Boisnard : "A charmer who knows how to be unpleasant"

A timekeeper for Matra, Tyrrell, then Renault, Anne Boisnard followed Alain Prost to McLaren in 1984. In the male environment that is Formula 1, her woman's viewpoint is of particular interest:
"Alain is intelligent and charming and you can see it in his eyes. But he also knows how to be unpleasant when he needs to be. He can be a Grumpy Frenchman and he can moan! But it is always in an attempt to get something better and he was often right. He really liked the way the English worked as it dovetailed perfectly with his punctilious nature. He was on the same wavelength as Ron Dennis in terms of always chasing after the tiny details. He got on well with his engineers and there was always a perfect understanding running through the team. But you know, that is one of Ron Dennis' great qualities that he can create a convivial atmosphere which is not always evident from the outside. People think he is sour tempered and unpleasant, but that's not true. He is like a pater familias who really looks after all his mechanics. He wants people to be contented. But he is hard and insists on a job well done. Everyone must be neat and tidy and Alain likes this very strict way of working. And when he asked for something he got it."

(Archives Anne Boisnard)

by former Brabham technical director, Gordon Murray. The new chassis was the equal of its predecessor in the MP4 lineage and if the TAG-Porsche V6 proved as reliable as in the past, even if it was not the most powerful, then why not dream of a third consecutive title?

Certainly the start of the 1987 championship seemed to support that argument. Prost triumphed in Brazil thanks to a classy drive that saw him look after his tyres and in Belgium, his rivals all fell by the wayside. The victory in Spa

was a big day for the Frenchman who equalled Jackie Stewart's long held record and the man himself was there at the Ardennes circuit to congratulate Prost. The next landmark came at Estoril, late in the season where Alain took his 28th Grand Prix victory to stand alone at the head of the wins table in Formula 1. Between these two races, he faced the facts: he would not be world champion in 1987. The Porsche had lost its famed reliability. Along with major mechanical failures, twopenny bit parts also let

• **83**_At the end of a cliff-hanger of a race, Alain Prost crossed the line to win in Adelaide in 1986 having told his on-board computer where to go. He became a double world champion one year after taking his first title, which is a very rare occurrence!

Designers: John Barnard and Steve Nichols

Same technical caracteristics then MP4/2C except:

Engine
Maximum power: 900 hp
Weight: 140 kg (without turbos, intercoolers or exhausts)

Dimensions
Wheelbase: 2794 mm
Track: 1841 mm (Front) / 1676 mm (Rear)

Used all season.

• **84**_TAG-McLaren was not doing so well in 1987 but the atmosphere was still good as can be seen at this far from dull evening with Odwin Podlech (Thierry Boutsen's manager,) Stefan Johansson, Alain Prost, Ron Dennis and Anne-Marie Prost. A few seconds after this photo was taken, Alain and Stefan got up and whipped the table cloth away. Boys will be boys!

go, such as an alternator belt that broke at Imola and Hockenheim, robbing the champion of a possible win in Italy and an almost definite one in Germany. In any case, it would not have been enough as this year, Nelson Piquet and his Williams calmly picked up a string of second places as he headed for the supreme title with all the diligent application of a conscientious artisan. In fact, Ron Dennis was giving serious thought to employing the "carioca" as a replacement for Stefan Johansson in 1988. Stefan was an excellent driver who got on perfectly well with Alain. *"Contrary to what you might expect, he was quite*

a funny guy and we had a good time together," but he was cruelly lacking in the scope required to be a great champion. Ron was determined to build another "dream team," just like the rewarding partnership between Lauda and Prost.

A storm was brewing in the summer of 1987. In the Honda camp, there was some disquiet about the electric atmosphere growing at Williams between Piquet and Mansell over the past two years and the partnership was beginning to sour. Naturally, the company made contact with McLaren and the decision was taken in mid-

August. Honda parted company with Williams at the end of the season and supplied the McLaren team as from the start of the 1988 season. As the fine print was being drawn up, Alain Prost suggested to the Japanese that he preferred Ayrton Senna to Nelson Piquet, who was also preparing to leave Williams. *"I was very close to Nelson, but once again, I always intended to adopt the role of a team player,"* recalls Alain. Just before the Italian Grand Prix, Ron Dennis put on a lavish media presentation to announce to the world's press in the gardens of a

park at the Monza circuit his new "dream team." There was no doubt that Ayrton Senna was ready to tackle the challenge of his life and Alain Prost was thinking back to 1984. Once again, a young ambitious driver was going to take on the experienced champion in a very closely contested duel. But this time, HE was the experienced champion and somewhere inside he knew he could eventually triumph over spirit and impulsiveness. He had no doubts, except that it would take him two years. ∎

• **85**_In the first round of 1987 in Rio, the "Professor" really lived up to his nickname, beating the quicker Williams through an excellent tyre choice and a clever pit stop strategy (two stops as against three for most of his rivals.) But the illusion did not last long.

• **86**_It's all in the detail: having dominated the German Grand Prix, Prost was robbed of victory on the final lap when the alternator belt on his Porsche V6 gave up the ghost. Adding insult to injury to his little mate's problems, Nelson Piquet, the delighted winner, gave Alain a lift back to the pits on the sidepod of his Williams.

Chapter 14
1988-1989
The incredible confrontation

● **88**_The greatest duel in history? There is no doubt that the Prost-Senna confrontation is one of the most incredible in the history of the world championship. In the first half of the 1988 season, Prost had the advantage, as can be seen here in the French Grand Prix where Alain suddenly pulled a surprise move at the Beausset double right, a corner he knew like the back of his hand, while Senna had hesitated for a fraction of a second behind a backmarker. After that, the roles would be reversed...

By bringing together Alain Prost and Ayrton Senna together under the one roof, Ron Dennis had put two roosters in the same barnyard. He was certainly not the first to have created such an explosive mixture and a few big bangs in the past had served to prove the limits of this type of alchemy. But events at McLaren in 1988 and 1989 would far exceed anything seen before in Formula 1 for intensity and drama. The doubts and uncertainties were to get the better of the sport in this merciless battle between the two greatest drivers it had seen over the past fifteen years and Alain's adventures over these two long seasons are best seen through a variety of perspectives (in order to better follow the chronology of events, it would be useful to refer to the work on Ayrton Senna, published in the same collection.)

Although it was obvious from the opening grands prix that the 1988 world champion would be driving a McLaren-Honda MP4-4, no one could foretell the extent to which the team would crush the opposition, cast adrift without any point of reference. The magnificent red and white cars won 15 of the 16 rounds! It meant that the final outcome would depend more on panache than the methodical approach. Alain

and Ayrton knew it would come down to the number of wins per driver. In the first half of the season, that is to say up to the French Grand Prix, Prost was in control, leading Senna by four wins to three and thus had a fifteen point lead. Despite everything, he had been very impressed, not to say surprised by the incredible involvement shown by his young team-mate who had the better of him in terms of pure speed in qualifying and Prost declared he did not intend getting into this particular fight. In 1984, he was the one who adopted the newcomer's role, up against the more experienced Lauda and he was sure history would repeat itself. But this time, the players and the environment were different.

Senna began the summer with a brilliant run of four wins in a row and Alain, apparently resigned to his fate, admitted publicly after the Belgian Grand Prix that his team-mate deserved the title because he was so committed. What had happened? Not much and yet quite a lot.

Prost emerged victorious in the French Grand Prix, having shown that he too could drive "like Senna." Then came the British Grand Prix and an episode that the media made a meal of and a scrappy one at that. The basics of the problem were clear: while Ayrton was mastering

the situation in the lead under a downpour at the Silverstone circuit, as usual one might add, Alain had slid back into the clutches of the pack almost immediately as his car was proving a handful in the rain. On lap 24 of 65, he came into the pits, undid his safety harness and without making excuses announced: *"it's my life and my decision. I decided there was nothing to be gained by continuing in these conditions."* He was vilified by those who felt a driver should never give up and defended by others who respected the decision of a champion who had won 32 grands prix. There is no doubt that this fear of driving in a fog of water in close company with other cars that are barely visible stemmed from the traumatic incident at Hockenheim in 1982. It is just as clear that this retirement constituted a sign of weakness in the image of Alain as a driver who, when up against a team-mate backed away from nothing to become the best of the best. *"Of course that day was a hard blow mentally,"* he confided recently. In terms of the sport he

had decided to miss out on ten points while still keeping the championship lead. Given the point made earlier regarding the total superiority of the McLarens, the decision was clearly very risky as the two drivers were so close that the driver had no more than one or two jokers to play. And Alain had just used one up. But surely Ayrton had also used one in Monaco. Now, the Frenchman was going to get it wrong on two more occasions, in Germany and Hungary. At both these races, he showed greater pace than his rival. But the problem was that in both cases he had to try and make up for a bad start and in fact a very bad start at the Hungaroring. He ended up having to try and come back after a spin in the rain in the first and then make up for a botched passing move in the other. He came away with two second places to add to the Silverstone no-score, followed by another third place in Belgium where the Frenchman was beaten in terms of pure speed. The writing was on the wall. Alain realised that he had

• **89_**After a sunny French Grand Prix, Alain Prost found himself shrouded in the rain at the British Grand Prix. Stumbling through the fog in the middle of a pack of second string cars, he was navigating round in 15th place. His McLaren was far from perfect so they say and he made the decision to retire on safety grounds. But his mental well-being was dealt a severe blow by fierce criticism in the press.

Designer: Steve Nichols

Engine

Make/Type: Honda RA 168-E
Number of Cylinders/Configuration: V6 (Rear)
Capacity: 1494 cc
Bore/Stroke: 79 x 50.8 mm
Compression ratio: 9.6: 1
Turbo(s): 2, IHI
Maximum power: Around 650 hp
Maximum revs: 12500 rpm
Block material: Cast alloy
Fuel/Oil: Shell
Sparking plugs: NGK
Injection: Honda/PGM-F1
Valve gear: 4 OHC
Number of valves per cylinder: 4
Ignition: Honda
Weight (without intercoolers): 150 kg

Transmission

Gearbox/Number of gears: McLaren (6)
Clutch: AP

Chassis

Type: Carbon monocoque
Suspensions: Wishbones, pullrods (Front), Double wishbones, pushrods (Rear)
Shock absorbers: Showa
Rim diameter: 13" (Front and Rear)
Rim width: 11.5" (Front) / 16.3" (Rear)
Tyres: Goodyear
Brakes: Brembo/SEP discs

Dimensions

Wheelbase: 2875 mm
Track: 1824 mm (Front) / 1640 mm (Rear)
Dry weight: 540 kg
Fuel capacity: 150 litres

Used all season.

underestimated his team-mate's incredible level of commitment at every level of the game without exception. Nevertheless, he pulled himself together and won the Spanish and Portuguese Grands Prix in quick succession, but he was quite simply crucified by a majestic Senna in Japan. *"Ite missa est!"* Prost clung onto his motivation to take a comfortable 35th win beating the new champion in the streets of Adelaide and the two men congratulated one another on the podium. Alain had to admit to the Brazilian's slight superiority in what had been a gentlemanly contest and Prost hoped that the following year, *"Ayrton would feel some of the pressure lift off him and be a bit more relaxed."* But in 1988, quite possibly the pressure was not exactly where people thought it was.

On the night of the fourth round of the 1989 championship, in Mexico, Alain Prost was frustrated. Not only had Senna not eased up, the Brazilian had totally crushed him in the last three races. More seriously, the atmosphere within the McLaren team had become unbearable. The big explosion came after Imola. On the Italian track, Senna broke the non-aggression pact at the first corner, a pact he had requested and that Prost had naively and logically adhered to. In order to pour oil on troubled waters, Ron Dennis summoned his two drivers during a test session at Pembrey in Wales. Locked away in the motorhome, Senna admitted he was at fault and apologised to his team-mate. He had tears in his eyes. It was clearly understood that this little chat was not to go any further than the four walls of the bus and this turned out to be the moment when Alain inadvertently lit the fuse to the powder keg.

The French sport's paper *L'EQUIPE* published an article by Johnny Rives a few days later with an account of what was said that day in Pembrey. Ayrton Senna was furious, felt humiliated and

from then on broke off relations with his team-mate. Was Prost trying to destabilise his rival psychologically? Many people think so, but Alain vehemently denies any such notion. *"If ever any idea was 200% wrong that's it! In fact, I was more destabilised than Ayrton because I found myself in a position of weakness and he was the one with a legitimate grievance. Johnny and me were great mates. I explained to him on the telephone what had happened after Imola, but completely off the record. I told him in confidence. And he wrote a story about it. It's the only time he betrayed my confidence and I really gave him a ticking off about it."* Johnny Rives is not in total agreement with this version of events. *"Alain did have a go at me for publishing the story, but sincerely, I cannot recall him telling me this in secret. He had already told me loads of things like this and I had respected his decision. And in this case, when he spoke about it being secret, I have my doubts. Because Alain can be*

astute and it meant he could cover his back as far as Ron Dennis was concerned. If I did really betray him, it was not intentional and I was not playing a trick on him." Whatever the truth, the damage was done. It would take four years of fierce fighting, sometimes to extremes for Alain and Ayrton to be seen sharing a joke in good heart; to be precise, on the night of the 1993 Australian Grand Prix.

As if this episode was not troubling enough for Alain Prost, there was also the matter of what he thought Honda felt about it (see sidebar.) This problem was much bigger and more complex than the previous one and it is well nigh impossible to reach a conclusion as to the truth behind it. At the start of 1989, Prost became more and more convinced that Senna was being favoured by the Japanese, that he got more of their attention, but above all he was being given better engines. He voiced his doubts in public and part of his French fan base immediately forgot

• **90_**While he had been written off by many after Senna's string of four wins in the summer of 1988, Prost then put the record straight by taking slick and precise wins in the Spanish (photo) and Portuguese Grands Prix. It put him back in the title race.

Was Alain Prost mistreated by Honda?

The controversy sparked by the French champion in 1989 has to this day not been resolved. Given that one can place the cursor of truth where one chooses on the line between the recriminations of a driver at one end and the underhanded actions of an engine supplier at the other, all one can do is listen to the opinions of those who are well informed, starting with the aggrieved party himself:

"It all began at the first test session in the MP4-4 at Imola, at the start of 1988. Ron wanted me to drive the car first. So I drove it and suggested that Ayrton have his turn so that we could share the programme. Ron told me to carry on. Then Ayrton began to pull a face and immediately I was thrown out of the car! I immediately went to see Ron: "you told me to try some things and I haven't finished." He said, "no don't worry, it's just that you've got to let him have a drive." That's when I got a flea in my ear and said to myself: "shit, it's going to be tough!" At the end of 1988, I had dinner with a very senior person at Honda who explained their choice to me: it was a question of different generations. They preferred Ayrton because he represented youth and he was full of spirit. This was never made public of course, because a manufacturer never admits to anything, but that evening this person apologised for this bias and not just in technical terms. 80% of a driver's armoury is mental and in this area it was impossible to fight on equal terms. However, there were engines with labels that read "Special for Senna." The problem is that as soon as one reveals something like this, people think you are looking for an excuse by attacking your opponent, which is not always the case. I always recognised Senna's qualities. My difficulty with McLaren was how to handle these qualities, the Honda problem and indirectly, the media side which to a certain extent favoured Ayrton, it has to be admitted." When questioned on the matter, the Honda person mentioned by Prost insisted only on saying that the way Prost had set out the facts "is not correct," without wishing to add anything else.

Johnny Rives also has an opinion and offers an interesting anecdote on the subject:

"I don't think Honda deliberately wished ill on Alain, or at least not at first. But Senna had such a hold on them through his powers of persuasion and his passion and by the interest he showed in the workings of the engines, that they were all crazy about him. After that, they might well have prepared special engines for Senna, thinking that he paid such close attention to everything on the engine side that it was worth giving him special parts or whatever else, I don't know. It soon became obvious that Senna had better engines. It was flagrant at Monza in 1989. Prost could not pass Berger by slipstreaming him, however, he won the race because Senna's engine blew up. At the start of the race, Ayrton was blowing him away! Ron Dennis then asked me to come to McLaren where Osamu Goto showed me Alain's speeds in the Parabolica and Lesmo. It was so ridiculous that I asked if they were joking or if they thought I was stupid. They wanted to make me believe that Alain was doing 170 km/h in the Parabolica, where everyone does 270 km/h and that explained why he was slow down the straight. I'm prepared to believe he was 5 km/h slower than Senna, but 80, no! If they had been dealing with a 19 year old kid who was just starting out as a journalist, then I could understand them bringing out an insult like this. Out of a sense of propriety I didn't even mention it in the newspaper, because I felt it was such a low thing to do." Steve Nichols, the designer of the McLaren MP4-4 gives us his personal opinion:

"If it did happen, it was done very discretely. I personally had no proof of it. Really, I can neither confirm nor deny it. Both Alain and Ayrton were excellent drivers and very close in performance terms. Every minute of the day, they thought about how to beat each other. It was really so intense. Alain knows McLaren as well as I do and, in any case, if Honda had done something like that, they would have kept it secret."

As can be seen, nothing can be confirmed one way or the other. Certain aspects of history could be discussed forever.

Designer: Neil Oatley

Engine
Make/Type: Honda RA 109-E
Number of Cylinders/Configuration: V10 (Rear)
Capacity: 3490 cc
Bore/Stroke: 92 x 52.5 mm
Compression ratio: not given
Maximum power: 675 hp
Maximum revs: 13000 rmp
Block material: Aluminium
Fuel/Oil: Shell
Sparking plugs: NGK
Injection: Honda/PGM-F1
Valve gear: 4 OHC
Number of valves per cylinder: 4
Ignition: Honda
Weight: not given

Transmission
Gearbox/Number of gears: McLaren (6)
Clutch: AP

Chassis
Type: Carbon monocoque
Suspensions: Wishbones, pullrods (Front), Double wishbones,
pushrods (Rear)
Shock absorbers: Showa
Rim diameter: 13" (Front and Rear)
Rim diameter: 12" (Front) / 16.3" (Rear)
Tyres: Goodyear
Brakes: Brembo/SEP discs

Dimensions
Wheelbase: 2896 mm
Track: 1820 mm (Front) / 1670 mm (Rear)
Dry weight: 500 kg
Fuel capacity: not given

Used all season.

● **91-92**_On the 1988
Australian Grand Prix podium
(on left) all's well that ends
well. Senna, the new world
champion and Prost his
acolyte, the winner on the
day celebrate a great year
spent monopolising the
victories. Five months later
at Imola (on right) they kept
their distance. Senna does
not hold back in celebrating
the win while Prost is unable
to deal with the double-cross
his team-mate dealt him on
the opening lap.

their love of a hero and accused him of being a
bad loser. *"I would rather be seen as a whiner
than an idiot,"* replied Alain at the time, showing
once again the dark side of his character. But
deep down inside, he knew that the good days
at McLaren had passed. He took matters into
his own hands, announcing at the French Grand
Prix that he intended leaving the team that had
given him everything, that had been his family,
but where he now felt like more and more of a
stranger. But he still had to finish the season and
his main priority was regaining his champion's
crown. Given the doubts he had regarding
favouritism from various parties, he was aware
that the road he travelled was about to become
even more dangerous.

Strangely enough, it was from this point on
that Prost inexorably began to break away from
Senna in the championship. He won in France
and England, where his rival failed to score. Then,
once back on the road to success, Alain picked up
a string of second places, not forgetting the art
of winning when Ayrton stumbled again, as he

did in Italy. Finally, his greater experience was
allowing him to control the misdirected
impetuousness of the young wolf. But not
quite the way Prost had hoped for, as the last
part of the season was very trying. Alain Prost
felt he had been pretty much abandoned by the
majority of the McLaren crew. *"It was incredible
what had to be done to battle against adversity.
In Monza, all the cars were set up for Ayrton.
Nothing worked properly in the pits and my
faithful mechanics looked really miserable.
All the power had switched to the other side of
the garage. That was really tough."* Despite or
because of his isolation within the team, Alain
Prost found the inner strength needed to fight on
alone. His rival had won more grands prix, but he
headed the classification going to Japan. On top
of that, he knew that Senna had to win in Suzuka
to keep his title hopes alive. With this in mind, he
had warned the Brazilian, via the media, that he
had no intention of leaving the door open.
Senna's swashbucking overtaking moves were
now legendary, but many were based on outright

• **93**_Railing against injustice! The French press made a meal of the new controversy stirred up in Imola. A few days later, a sensational story would ignite the powder keg!
(*L'EQUIPE newspaper archive*)

• **94**_Winning in the States in 1989 should have made Alain Prost happy, as he had never been at ease on the American street circuits. On top of that, he was back in the lead of the world championship. But the growing tension within McLaren took away the pleasure. He knew he owed this win to a mechanical failure on Senna's car and became ever more suspicious that Honda was showing signs of partiality.

intimidation that had sometimes got the better of Alain. He therefore decided that from now on, he would stand firm.

Leading the race on the Japanese circuit, Prost was controlling the situation, even if he knew Ayrton was closing on him with each passing lap. For some time, the Frenchman had realised it was better to prepare his car for the race than to embark on a vain contest for pole against the man he admitted was better than him in qualifying. On this day, his car was perfect and he knew Senna would be unable to pass him given the narrow nature of the Suzuka track. Braking for the Casio chicane, he usually took a line that prevented anyone from coming up the inside. So, when he looked to his right and saw the nose of the No. 1 McLaren, he was rather surprised. *"As I had not seen him in my mirrors before the corner, in my mind, it was impossible that he could be there a fraction of a second later. Therefore, instead of taking what one could call a pure "qualifying" line, I took more of a*

• **95_** *"Alain don't leave us, we still need you here," seems to be Ron Dennis' message to Alain Prost in June 1989. "Ron offered me an extension to my contract," recalls Alain today. "But I was well aware why. This pairing suited him very well, even if it was hard to manage. I did all the development testing over the winter. He would ring me during the week sometimes, asking me to come to England urgently because Ayrton was stuck in Brazil. Once or twice, that was alright, but after that…!"* Prost announced he was leaving McLaren at the French Grand Prix. Alain and Ron had built up a strong personal relationship over the past four years. When Dennis learnt his driver was moving to "the enemy," Ferrari, he saw red!

"race" line, a hairsbreadth more to the right and that was all. But given where he was, at the speed he was travelling, maybe 8 or 9 km/h quicker than usual, I could not avoid him. Contrary to what one might believe, I was disappointed. People think I was looking to crash into him. That's wrong, I really wanted to win the race because my car was capable of it. Ayrton was really on the limit behind me. I let him close a bit because I was nowhere near the limit that day. I was planning to pull away again to break his will." The collision ended with both cars stuck in the escape road and Prost calmly stepped from the cockpit without even glancing at the Brazilian. But Senna frantically made every effort imaginable to try and win the race at all costs. By then, Alain was already up in race control where he went through what happened with FISA President Jean-Marie Balestre. In the end, Senna was disqualified for three irrefutable misdemeanours, so Alain Prost thus came by his third world championship crown.

At the time, given the acrimonious circumstances of the 1989 season, this seemed like the least commendable of the three won by the Frenchman. With hindsight, it has a special dimension and a worth which cannot be denied. While it was obvious that Prost was not the most brilliant driver on track that year, it is equally clear that he was the strongest mentally and the most psychologically sound. He took the supreme prize battling not only his rival, but also his team, his engine supplier

and to a certain extent, public opinion! Thus ended six long years spent with a team where he learnt an efficient and practical way of working. It would prove to be damned useful in his new venture. ■

● **96**_Adelaide 1989: The race where Prost proved he was right. The weather was so diabolical that it seemed reasonable to delay the start of the race. Pretty much all the drivers were in agreement. Under pressure from sponsors, television and their teams, they all meekly got into their cars. Alain completed the first lap so that the team could pick up the start money, having proved on the way that he had the measure of Senna in the rain (photo) before retiring in a gesture of protest. Given the number of crashes that followed one after the other, including one for Senna, almost all the drivers ruefully agreed that Prost had been the only one to make the sensible decision that day.

Chapter *15*
1990
Life in the red

Designer: John Barnard/Ferrari Design Team

Engine

Make/Type: Typo 036/037
Number of Cylinders/Configuration: V12 (Rear)
Capacity: 3497.9 cc
Bore/Stroke: 84.0 x 52.6 mm
Compression ratio: 12.5:1
Maximum power: 685 hp
Maximum revs: 13000 rpm
Block material: Fonte
Fuel/Oil: Agip
Sparking plugs: Champion
Injection: Magneti Marelli/Weber
Valve gear: 4 ACT
Number of valves per cylinder: 5
Ignition: Magneti Marelli
Weight: not communicated

Transmission

Gearbox/Number of gears: Ferrari (7)
Clutch: AP

Chassis

Type: Carbon monocoque
Suspension: Double wishbone, pushrods, torsion bar and inboard
Front damper; double wishbone, pushrod-spring and inboard Front
damper
Shock absorbers: Penske
Rim diameter: 13" (Front and Rear)
Rim width: 11.75" (Front) / 16.3" (Rear)
Tyres: Goodyear
Brakes: Brembo/SEP with discs

Dimensions

Wheelbase: 2880 mm
Track: 1800 mm (Front) / 1680 mm (Rear)
Dry weight: 500 kg
Fuel capacity: not communicated

Used all season.

Even if unprepared to admit it, every Formula 1 driver dreams of working for the most prestigious team, the only one that has been here since 13th May 1950 at Silverstone for the first ever Grand Prix counting towards the Drivers' World Championship. The team has more- titles than any other and is of course Scuderia Ferrari. Every driver also knows he will have to deal with politics Italian-style, with intrigue in the air and gossip in the corridors. A clear state of mind is essential when working for the Prancing Horse stable. Alain Prost weighed up the pros and cons during the summer of 1989 and felt ready to accept a proposition from Ferrari's sporting director, Cesare Fiorio. *"We first got in touch on a very informal basis, notably on the golf course,"* recalls Cesare. *"And then we were able to draw up a proposal at the 1989 German Grand Prix at Hockenheim, on Friday after practice. Of course it was in secret as it had to be that way. We pretty much went through every point between the two of us, without the help of dozens of lawyers as is the case these days. Then we met again, still in secret, in Sardinia where I had a yacht and that is where we actually signed the definitive contract."*

Ferrari was in great need of Prost. The most legendary Formula 1 team was struggling to capture the glory days of yesteryear and despite taking on big name designers such as Harvey Postlewaithe and John Barnard, could not drag itself out of a mire of mediocrity that had held it fast for the past few years. The last constructors' title dated back to 1983, while Jody Scheckter had been the last man to bring them the drivers' crown in 1979. When he came onboard at the start of 1989, Cesare Fiorio soon realised that his drivers, Nigel Mansell and Gerhard Berger had excellent qualities, but they were lacking a vital ingredient in that they were not the sort to build things around them nor were they leaders of men. As far as the elegant Italian was concerned, there were only two drivers in the Formula 1 field who fitted the bill. And one of them was going through a state of disgrace with his team. Prost also had something of a need for Ferrari. Even if

• **98-99**_His 1990 victory on the beautiful and newly remodelled Interlagos circuit was a source of great joy for Alain Prost. It was his sixth win in Brazil, (a record) a first with Ferrari, the 100th in the Scuderia's history and above all, he was winning in front of Senna's naturally partisan home crowd who had booed him all weekend. Let joy be unconfined.

he had taken the title, the Frenchman had
endured a painful end to the year when he was
spared nothing. Very much aware of his own self-
image, he was not happy with the impression he
made in 1989. He felt that the Scuderia was
treading water and he had pretensions about
turning it around. If he pulled off this impressive
feat, he would be remembered forever as THE
driver who had restored glory to Ferrari. Alain
was therefore teamed up with Nigel Mansell. The
two men had known one another for a while and
respect was mutual, but in fact, they knew very
little about the other. Stuck together in the same
team, they would soon learn!

John Barnard quit Ferrari when Alain Prost
arrived. The Frenchman counteracted this
difficulty by suggesting to the management of
the august team that they take on Steve Nichols.
The American's efforts were centred on improving
the reliability of Barnard's Ferrari 641. After an
initial faux pas in the streets of Phoenix, the
reward came in Sao Paulo, Ayrton Senna's home
town. Even if this victory which came about
because of a collision between the leader Senna
and Nakajima, was rather a lucky one, it was
good to have. It gave a boost to what would be a
fascinating season for the whole team that was

already wrapped up in its new messiah. Alain had
just pointed the way to the top. But more than
that, the Frenchman was definitively adopted by
an entire nation: his charisma, the fact he spoke
Italian and this first win confirmed his status as
the saviour of a national treasure. The signs of
promise seen in Brazil took a long time to
materialise. In the next three events, the men in
red were hit with a variety of problems and Alain
had to settle for a few crumbs from the table.
The Frenchman's main concern was the Goodyear
qualifying tyres, which he found very difficult to
get to grips with. *"I always had problems with
qualifying tyres, even at McLaren. I think it was
down to my driving style that was a bit too
smooth. If you don't heat up the tyres in the first
few corners and you try to get the car to slide, it
damages the tyres."* When Alain only qualified
13ᵗʰ on the grid in Mexico, while Mansell was 4ᵗʰ,
even his most fervent fans became sceptical. The
man himself stayed calm and announced to his
incredulous team that he was going to win the
race! *"Right from Friday, I had an inkling. I was
going almost as quick with 60 litres of fuel on
race tyres as I did on light tanks with qualifying
tyres! Once I'd taken that onboard, I spent all of
Saturday fine tuning the car for the race. And I*

Steve Nichols: "He brought a more disciplined approach to Ferrari"

Having worked in the United States for a damper manufacturer in Indycar, Steve Nichols joined McLaren at the end of 1980 and stayed until the end of 1989, when he followed Alain Prost to Ferrari to become the new technical director. He spoke to us about the champion's influence on the team:

"I think that when he arrived at Ferrari, Alain was a legend. When he said, " we have to do this to the engine," or "we must do this to the chassis," the people would do it. He was quite staggering when it came to the precision of his set-up on the chassis. To give you an example, at that time, Ferrari provided suspension springs with a rating that varied in gradations of 10% with gaps of 100 pounds per inch. He wanted 25 pounds per inch, or 2.5%. He always chased the smallest detail which allowed him to make a difference. He was also equally demanding when it came to the engines and could spend hours testing different blocks and assessing their endurance. He really wanted to get the car we were hoping for. His talent could obviously not do anything about a bad car and with that in mind he was always pushing us to improve the car and to strive for perfection. In 1990 we made significant progress. We managed to take a car that could not finish one race out of two the previous year and make it reliable. In fact, while we did lose, it did not happen until Suzuka remember. But for that regrettable collision, I am convinced he could have taken the title."

• **102**_The "professor" at work in Mexico: *"It was one of the happiest moments of my racing career! At the start it was a bit difficult to overtake, but the car settled down after two or three laps and then I began passing the others and it was great fun! It was not easy to manage, because in this situation the tendency is to try and go too quickly to catch up with the leaders who are already a long way ahead."*

Cesare Fiorio : "Mansell had to give best to Prost"

Part of the Fiat court, Cesare Fiorio, known as "Hollywood" for his love of the flash and his sunglasses permanently perched on his nose, was the sporting director of the Lancia Rally team before joining Ferrari in 1989. He was really impressed by Alain Prost:

"Above all, it was his mental strength that struck me. Mansell was a great champion, with an extraordinary natural talent, but when he came up against Alain's mental capacity, I would say he looked very small. I can remember one incident at the Brazilian Grand Prix. The drivers swapped views on set-up, wings, suspension, dampers and so forth. The collaboration seemed good, at least on the outside. On the grid, Alain's car was next to Nigel's. With five minutes to go, Alain called over the mechanics to make a couple of changes. He did not change much, but gave Nigel the impression that he was changing the whole set-up at the last moment. Nigel went crazy! He wanted to know what was going on and wanted the same thing. But it was too late the race was underway. He had to give best to Alain's tactical intelligence all year long. Alain won five races and Nigel one, even though they had the same equipment.

He was a real champion. He was quicker than the others and made fewer mistakes. All team managers admire these qualities in the drivers they run. He was quick, intelligent and understood tactics, so all the elements of success were in place. His faults? I'd say that from a technical point of view he did not like racing in the rain much. He was no slower than the others, but he did not feel comfortable. The other fault was maybe his relationship with the team could have been better, but that is the way he is. He was a bit cold and not everyone's idea of a mate. But then, while everyone's mate might be better liked he doesn't move things forward. Better a cold fish who goes quickly."

qualified 13th on race tyres. I was sure it was going to be alright the next day as I had set up the car perfectly." There is little doubt that on that Sunday 24th June Prost drove one of the most incredible races of his career. It demanded respect. The "professor" set off cautiously to avoid mishap and to get a feel for his car. Once confident in his Ferrari, he gradually stepped up the pace and moved up the order lap by lap. While maintaining concentration, Alain was having a whale of a time overtaking his colleagues who had not expected to see him that day. Everyone had to give best, Berger, Piquet, Alesi, Mansell and Patrese. Only Senna, out in front in the lead had not yet felt the fury of the tornado. On lap 61, after harrying the Brazilian for ten laps, Prost got past and the deed was done. Alain was in the lead, never to give it up. The triumph was complete thanks to an heroic second place for Mansell. Two rounds later, after the British Grand Prix, Alain Prost had become the hero of Italy. He had just taken two wins in a row after the one in Mexico, at Paul Ricard and Silverstone which saw him knock Senna off the top of the classification. By the mid-point of the 1990 season, he had won four of eight races and many pundits felt that the three times world champion was on the verge of pulling off a difficult gamble. From now on, Alain was the centre of attention both within and outside the team and his popularity has reached its zenith.

The future looked bright and shiny, but unfortunately it tarnished in the second half of the season. First off, Senna and McLaren reacted with their expected efficiency and the Ferraris dropped back with every passing grand prix. Despite it all, Prost managed to hang onto the Brazilian's coat tails, but Mansell lost all his motivation, put out by his team-mate's status within the team and he even announced he was planning to retire at the end of the season. His performance dropped off and Fiorio was determined to replace him during the season with the team's young test driver, Gianni Morbidelli. Perturbed by having a team-mate who contributed nothing to the team, Alain supported his sporting director's initiative. But the Fiat bosses were against evicting "a great champion" and the moustachioed one saved his place in the Scuderia, but he saved neither the Scuderia nor Alain Prost!

The Portuguese Grand Prix was crucial for the reds. In qualifying, the Ferrari 641 outperformed the McLarens and Mansell was on pole with Prost alongside him. Yet again, the Frenchman had set up his car for the race and told anyone who would listen that his car was perfect. He really needed to win here to get back in touch with Senna. Team orders therefore dictated that Mansell do nothing that might impede his team-mate. However, come the start, the Englishman made such a good job of

spinning his wheels that he lost control and slammed his incredulous team-mate into the pit wall. Alain had to back off and found himself fifth. He was in a complete rage! *"I'm sure what Mansell did at the start was not intentional,"* explains Cesare today. *"He made a mistake, losing control of the car which meant that both cars had to slow down. The result was that both McLarens and Piquet got ahead. A driver, even if he's a bit mad, doesn't do that."* Alain does not agree at all. *"I am sure it was intentional. The problem is that there is what you see on the screen and what you see from inside the car. You can see the eyes looking at you in the mirrors. Quite simply, he did not want me to be world champion in the same car as him in the same team."* Whatever the truth, the Frenchman had to knuckle down and managed to get up to third place at the end of the event, while his team-mate had taken the lead. At that point the race was red flagged following an accident. The result was therefore: 1st Mansell, 2nd Senna and 3rd Prost. Fiorio and Mansell congratulated one another and Alain saw red again. He sternly criticised his technical director for this inappropriate behaviour and furious, declared that Ferrari did not deserve to take the championship title! All the hard work and bridge building of the past months was going down the drain. Prost was now 18 points down on Senna with three rounds to go and he was sick at what he saw as a waste. At Fiat, it

seemed the bosses shared his view and once back in Italy, Giovanni Agnelli banged the table. Reason had to be restored and the fight had to be taken to the bitter end. The next weekend, the Ferraris were untouchable at Jerez and Mansell wisely let his team-mate move into the lead after a pit stop and then did an efficient job of blocking Senna. On the podium, Alain and Nigel congratulated one another, but the smiles were just a façade. The Frenchman had no time for the Englishman, who in any case knew that a nice warm seat awaited him at Williams for the following year, after he had shelved his plans to retire.

After qualifying for the Japanese Grand Prix at the Suzuka circuit, Alain Prost was confident nevertheless. Senna took pole position, but unfortunately was on the dirty side of the track on the right, which put him into a right old rage, while Prost was on the clean side. In recent weeks, the Ferrari chassis had made enormous progress and had the legs of the McLaren, as could be seen with wins in Portugal and Spain. Alain was therefore convinced that, if he could get away in the lead into the fast right after the pits, he had every chance of winning the grand prix. Senna knew it too. As soon as the green light came on, the Ferrari shot away down the hill leading to the famous corner. Prost had stayed on the left hand side of the track, but very quickly closed the open door to take up his line

● **104_**"As planned" Alain Prost triumphed at Jerez. The Scuderia had applied an effective strategy which made up in part for missing out big time in Estoril a week earlier.

• **105**_Suzuka 1990. The green light has just come on and in a few seconds, the clash would occur 500 metres further on. On the right, Ayrton Senna's McLaren scrabbles in the dust while Alain Prost's Ferrari makes an impeccable getaway. But the power of the Honda V10 allows the Brazilian to catch up with his enemy as they approach the first turn and he punts him off the track. One year later...

for the corner when he suddenly felt the back end break away. He tried desperately to straighten up, but soon realised he could do nothing about it. He had lost his rear wing and his race was all over, almost before it began, in the gravel trap, accompanied by Senna's McLaren. The Brazilian had deliberately run into the back of the Ferrari, so the grand prix and the championship was over. Ayrton Senna was world champion. A few minutes later, the two men walked back to the pits in silence. While Ayrton

disdainfully denied any responsibility for the collision, he invoked the idea of revenge for what had happened here a year earlier. Alain was livid. A few weeks earlier in Monza, the two rivals produced an historic handshake which was supposed to put an end to this nasty hidden war that was harming the image of the sport. Believing this rapprochement to be genuine, Prost was even more aghast and said that if racing had come to this, then it was not for him. He spoke of retirement and the wound was deep.

Apart from this disconsolate final scene, the 1990 season was still something of a success for Alain Prost and his team. Not since the era of the sainted Niki Lauda had the Scuderia won six grands prix in the year. The Frenchman had been able to galvanise the entire team towards the single goal of victory and he is still nostalgic about those days. *"They were not stars, they were not the best, nor the most experienced, but they had a real will to win. The way we worked was impeccable. Up to*

the Portuguese Grand Prix, given the way we had optimised things, I have no hesitation in saying it was a fantastic year." A fantastic year that ended with a heavy question mark hanging over Alain Prost's motor sport future. The driver did not wish to comment and took off for a few weeks holiday to give it all some thought, away from the attention of the media. Would his passion for racing prove stronger than his growing dislike of so many aspects of the sport. ∎

…at the same track, Senna openly admitted he did it on purpose to avenge the "humiliation" inflicted on him by Jean-Marie Balestre in 1989.

Chapter 16
1991–1992
Humiliation and renaissance

• **107**_In 1991, Prost found it very difficult to put his point across to the press who were hounding him. He accused them of bending his words and stirring things up. *"The problems with Ferrari at the time was that the newspapers were spread out on the desk in the morning and decisions were taken on what had been written. The first year, I was the saviour, the second, I was Alain Prost, alone and not at all supported by the team. You need a lot of experience to deal with that and at the time I did not have enough."*

During the winter of 90-91, Alain Prost had several discussions with the Fiat and Ferrari management. He wanted to start from scratch and find the inner peace needed to get into gear once more. He had deliberately put the bitterness of the previous year behind him and had turned his mind to more positive matters. He had taken an active role in winter testing and rediscovered the joy of driving. The arrival of his new team-mate, the young and ambitious Jean Alesi, raised hopes of a more peaceful coexistence than with Mansell. But given the way the Scuderia was going about its business, there did not seem to be much room for optimism.

The first problem was the car itself. Contrary to what Alain had hoped for, a new car was not on the way. Enrique Scalabroni and Henri Durand, respectively head of design and head of aerodynamics had left the team in the middle of the previous season, leaving Steve Nichols high and dry. Fiorio therefore decided to evolve the 641 into the 642B, with plans to introduce a new model later in the year. On top of that, because of a new rule governing the constituents of the fuel, Ferrari's supplier Agip had nothing new to offer and actually had to take a step backwards to conform to the rule, contrary to all the other

fuel companies. The result of this was that the V12 was actually down on power compared to 1990. Therefore it does not take a genius to work out what happened in 1991. What had been a superb squad, capable of taking the runner up position in the 1990 championship, spiralled down to the ranks of also-rans for 1991, up against McLaren and Williams. Right from the opening grands prix it became clear that not only would Alain Prost not be in the hunt for the title, but also that he would find it extremely difficult to fiddle home a few wins. In fact, for the first time in a decade, that's to say since he joined Renault, Alain would not record a single victory! When the 643 finally turned up in the course of the year, it brought a small positive evolution, but not enough to face up to the finely honed English rivals. All these technical difficulties paved the way for the Frenchman to experience at first hand the devastating effects of the underhand political scheming and other sordid settling of scores.

The first head to roll was Cesare Fiorio's. *"My personal situation with the then president of Ferrari, Piero Fusaro, had deteriorated a lot. Fusaro did not have a sports background, but was a bureaucrat parachuted into the role by*

Fiat. When there was that little problem in Portugal with Alain, a problem we would have worked round in my opinion, he tried to invent some sort of thing between us and he succeeded." Succeeded to such an extent that everyone was convinced that Prost had demanded and got the head of his sporting director. *"Never,"* Prost insists to this day. *"I would say to the journalists, 'stop it, I never asked for this. But they stuck with their own version of events as it sells papers and that's the way the system works."* Cesare backs up the manipulation theory. *"I don't think he asked for me to go. The proof is that everything was going well with Alain, but when I was running Ligier and then Briatore sold the team to Alain, everyone saw that I was gone in a fortnight. What was I supposed to do? Stay two years with him? So, what people were saying was wrong. Fusaro had used us for his personal ends. He destroyed everything Alain and I had built together. We had brought the team back to a very high level and it took just one incompetent to destroy it all."* Separated by events, Alain and Cesare went their separate ways and would not meet again for a while, by which time they realised to what extent they had been just pawns in the game.

The second head to roll belonged to none other than Alain Prost himself. The 1991 season was coming to an end in a dismal atmosphere and everyone could not wait to put it behind them and get on with 1992. Alain complained more and more often in the press about mistakes in the way the team was run, both in racing and human terms and thus carelessly laid himself open to attack from his enemies, as he would soon learn to his cost. At the same time, he had long meetings with the Scuderia's lawyer, Henry Peter, on the subject of a possible reorganisation of the team. Essentially, he wanted to be more involved in the way the team was run, while still staying in the cockpit. It was a problem in the cockpit that was going to get him into trouble at the Suzuka circuit at the penultimate round of the championship. Alain felt a stiff point in the steering column having thumped over a kerb and finished fourth with his arms in spasm from the effort. Quizzed by Italian television, he compared the steering of his Ferrari to that of a truck! As far as the Ferrari management was concerned this was totally unacceptable. The Frenchman reckons it was just too good a chance for them to miss and they dealt from the bottom of the pack. *"They latched onto the slightest pretext and*

• **108**_Everything went wrong at Ferrari in 1991. The arrival of the 643 in time for the French Grand Prix had been much awaited, but it did not bring the expected level of improvement. On the Magny-Cours track, Mansell and his Williams pointed out its shortcomings to Prost in this unrepeatable passing move at the Adelaide hairpin.

Designers: Steve Nichols/Ferrari Design Team

Engine
Make/Type: F1/91
Number of Cylinders/Configuration: V12 (Rear)
Capacity: 3499.2 cc
Bore/Stroke: 86.0 x 50.2 mm
Compression ratio: 12.5:1
Maximum power: 710 hp
Maximum revs: 13500 rpm
Block material: Fonte
Fuel/Oil: Agip
Sparking plugs: Champion
Injection: Magneti Marelli/Weber
Valve gear: 4 ACT
Number of valves per cylinder: 5
Ignition: Magneti Marelli
Weight: not communicated

Transmission
Gearbox/Number of gears: Ferrari (7)
Clutch: AP

Chassis
Type: Carbon monocoque
Suspension: Wishbones, pushrods (Front and Rear)
Shock absorbers: not communicated
Rim diameter: not communicated
Rim width: not communicated
Tyres: Goodyear
Brakes: Carbone Industrie/Brembo

Dimensions
Wheelbase: not communicated
Track: 1810 mm (Front) / 1678 mm (Rear)
Dry weight: not communicated
Fuel capacity: not communicated

Raced from France to Australia.

sadly, I supplied them with it. I never said my Ferrari was a truck, I said that its steering was as heavy as that on a truck. But then, at the trial, when we wanted to show the film of the interview, it was impossible to find it again. Strange don't you think?" Trial? Yes, for unfair dismissal and for breaking a contract before its term. Three days after making these rash remarks, the triple world champion, the man who had brought Ferrari back on the road to success was unceremoniously kicked out the door and replaced by Gianni Morbidelli for the final race of the season in Adelaide. Added to the displeasure of a mediocre season was the humiliation of being sacked and it rankled.

Finally, the third man to bite the dust was Piero Fusaro. A fortnight after the end of the season the fire-raising fireman was handed his hat and sent packing. In a replay of events of 1973, Giovanni Agnelli called up Luca Cordero di Montezemolo to come and get the team back on course. The elegant Roman immediately got in touch with Alain Prost and begged him to accept a

full apology from the Scuderia and asked him to come back. Alain respected Luca and knew him to be more than capable. But he had grown tired of it all and he already had another very interesting proposal to consider. He therefore politely turned down the offer and an amiable arrangement was reached between the two parties.

For the second time in his career, the first one dating back to 1983, Alain Prost found himself out on the streets at a time when all the hotels had shut for the night. But not quite all of them: hearing the news, Guy Ligier grabbed the nearest microphone to announce to the hapless out of work driver that he was welcome to join the Blues. However, with Thierry Boutsen and Erick Comas, his driver line-up was complete, but if Alain Prost wanted to do him the honour of driving one of his cars next year, then everyone would shuffle up a bit! Far from turning down this offer, which many believed was beneath him, Alain tested the Ligier JS37 powered by the Renault V10. *"Really, it wasn't that bad. The record I had set at Ricard at the time*

has never been beaten. I think this car, with a bit of development, especially in terms of its damping and aero package of course could have been competitive." But Prost would never race a Ligier. Guy offered a drive, but Alain wanted the car AND the team. Officially, discussions ground to a halt on this point after a long period of suspense that lasted right up to the start of the 1992 season. Ligier stated he was not yet ready to hand over the reins and Prost would not settle for just being the driver, or at least not with the Ligier team, although he kept that last thought to himself. But the basic problem was far more complex than it appeared and ten years on, neither Guy Ligier nor Alain Prost are keen to dwell on the subject.

Just as the Ligier route was buried forever, Prost was on the verge of being signed up by Williams-Renault. Talks had begun as soon as he was sacked from Ferrari. Renault saw the dream opportunity of finally getting "its" driver back, the man with whom they had to deal with the unfinished business of the 1983 season and for

Frank Williams, "it was obvious that Alain would contribute to us having an incredibly strong team." As far as Prost himself was concerned, he could see himself joining the strongest team at that time which would allow him to rebuild his reputation in style, with say a world championship title for example. There was no way he could drive for the team in 1992 but a contract for 1993 and 1994 was signed in secret as early as March. One notable clause that Alain had insisted on including, stated that Ayrton Senna could not join the driver line-up while he was there. When news broke that Mansell was to be replaced by Prost during the summer of 1992, raising the obvious question as to who would be his team-mate, Ayrton naturally offered his services. Finding out that this avenue was blocked, the Brazilian flew into one of his typical rages and ironically "welcomed" his rival back to the track! Once the Williams contract had been signed, Prost set about organising his sabbatical year in a workmanlike way. He needed to keep busy while also preparing for 1993. In order to

● **109**_Problems with the steering in Japan in 1991 came out all wrong when Prost tried to explain them. He paid the price.

Gérard Ducarouge: "He didn't brake!"

Technical director at Ligier in 1992, Gérard Ducarouge had never worked with Alain Prost, even though he had known him for a long time. During the first test session at the Paul Ricard circuit in early 1992, he therefore had the opportunity to see that Alain's reputation had not been blown up out of all proportion.

"We had done a lot of work on the car with adjustments specifically made at his request and, straightaway, he put in some fantastic lap times! It meant that thanks to all the data we took on board, I was able to see fundamental differences with other drivers. For example, the way he came into the return loop after the pits: he did not touch the brakes! But he was still reaching this point very quickly. That's what made the difference with the other drivers, even those with other teams present that day. So we instantly had to take off the brake cooling ducts and to cover up the self-cooling holes in the hubs with adhesive foil because the brakes were not getting up to temperature. It was unbelievable! Boutsen, who was driving the car in the afternoon, was the complete opposite. We had to put the large cooling ducts back on wide open. He was calm in the way he explained things. I saw Ayrton react in a much more instinctive way. Alain was more thoughtful and steadier. Everything was based on reason and he never rushed into anything, even when things weren't going well. He was totally at home in the role of a driver trying to make his team move forward, totally concentrated and giving everything his full attention. He would not stop until he had found the solution. He was totally implicated in the technical process, sometimes to an extreme degree. Ayrton was like that too."

• **111**_In a virgin white race suit and one of Erick Comas' helmets, Alain Prost tested the Ligier in January at Paul Ricard. Guy Ligier assumed the deal was done given the driver's positive comments on the car, but Prost insisted his role would not be restricted to driving. That is where the deal fell through.

keep up with the racing scene, he accepted an offer to commentate on the races live on French television. Then, in order to keep in shape physically, he took up cycling. The knee-torturing world of running was off limits as far as his physio Pierre Balleydier was concerned, so he had to take the plunge and jump on a hard saddle with pedals and two wheels attached. Cycling had never caught his imagination, but now it captivated him to such an extent that, even today he takes part in competitive events, some of which make use of stages on the Tour de France. In between weekends at the grands prix and arduous sessions in the saddle, he took plenty of time off to recharge his batteries, to clear his mind of all the mental turmoil and baggage he had picked up over the past few seasons. ∎

Chapter 17
1993
A comeback and farewell to glory

• **115**_An intense South African battle on the Professor's comeback in 1993. On the new Kyalami layout, Senna led from the start, but he was soon being harried by Prost who was as tactical as ever and who got past on lap 23. Further back, Schumacher watches before trying a similar move on the Brazilian, which resulted in a spin for the young German.

"I didn't pay much attention to the engine, it was so good. It was very driveable, especially this version and it was just what one needed when getting back behind the wheel. The chassis was phenomenal, it made the bumps disappear! I was so confident in it that after two or three corners, I took the straight behind the pits completely flat out even though it was damp and there was the odd puddle of water." That is what Alain Prost remembers of his first drive in the Williams-Renault FW14B at the Estoril circuit in September 1992. At the time, he had not driven for seven months and he was desperately keen to get as many miles under his belt as possible. He also got to know his team-mate better, who turned out to be Damon Hill, the son of the late Graham and also his team. Although they both share the same ideas when it comes to total commitment to winning, Williams Grand Prix and McLaren International are very different. In the case of Ron Dennis there is a certain human warmth which is not always evident to outsiders, whereas Frank Williams' team gives off a cool rigidity. Alain soon realised there was a limit to his relations with Frank, but on the

other hand, he heartily embraced the idea of discussions with technical director Patrick Head and his team. It did not take him long to feel the pressure from the media, who had latched onto the idea of this new challenge.

At the start of 1993, Renault did everything in its power to position Prost with the French press as the outright favourite for the world title. Some people maintained it was already in the bag, given the evident superiority of these cars with their active suspension and Renault V10 engine that had allowed Mansell to lap two seconds quicker than his rivals, including Senna in 1992! The general consensus was that if the Englishman could do that, then what could be expected of Prost, although this thought went unspoken. Naturally, there was another side to this media frenzy. If he failed, it would be open season for the driver, who would be the only one to blame if things went wrong. It turned out that the 1993 FW15 was far less forgiving to drive than the previous year's 14. "The 15 was more complex," recalls Alain, but with some terrible faults. It could be unpredictable, the rear suspension was not as good so traction suffered

and the cockpit was more complicated. On the older car you could really feel the active suspension working while with the new one, it was very stiff because it had to be made like that to work properly. Even Patrick admitted it was not as good. That meant we got the old one out a couple of times at Silverstone to do some back-to-back testing. It's the type of thing you have to be careful about, because it doesn't do the designers' ego much good. We persevered saying we would improve the new one, but the amount of progress was only marginal."

Fortunately, those who expected Prost to win every race were proved wrong. Indeed, the championship was undecided for much longer than had been expected. The return of "the Prostfessor" (as seen on a banner in the crowd at the Kyalami circuit) went off like a dream in South Africa, but then the Brazilian and European Grands Prix threw a spanner in the well oiled works. Because of a misunderstanding on the radio, Prost was unable to control his slick-shod Williams as it slid off in a downpour that hit both Interlagos and Donington and the team had to

Frank Williams: "Good to watch"

Although he ran one of the most successful teams in Formula 1, Frank Williams had not really had the chance to meet Alain Prost on a professional level.
"I think the first time I spoke with Alain about the possibility of him driving for me was in 1992. Up to then, we had some informal discussions in the Eighties, but at that time he was too involved at McLaren. He really did a good job for us. I think he also taught Damon a lot, which paid off for us later. He always wanted to drive and to win comfortably without too much effort. He had great mechanical sympathy with his car, he understood it and he never pushed it harder than he needed. But in qualifying, if Damon was pushing or if Ayrton was really threatening, he was capable of pushing the car to its furthest limit. If you watched him closely through the corners, you could see he was very smooth even when the car was in a four wheel drift. It was great to watch."

Designer: Adrian Newey

Engine

Make/Type: Renault RS5
Number of Cylinders/Configuration: V10 / (Rear)
Capacity: 3493 cc
Bore/Stroke: not communicated
Compression ratio: not communicated
Maximum power: 780 hp
Maximum revs: 14900 rpm
Block material: Aluminium
Fuel/Oil: Elf
Sparking plugs: Champion
Injection : Directe essence
Valve gear: 4 ACT
Number of valves per cylinder: 4
Ignition: Magneti Marelli
Weight: 135 kg

Transmission

Gearbox/Number of gears: Williams (6)
Clutch: AP

Chassis

Type: Carbon monocoque
Shock absorbers: Williams
Rim diameter: O.Z Wheels 13" (Front and Rear)
Rim width: O.Z Wheels 11.5" (Front) 13.7" (Rear)
Tyres: Goodyear 25.5"x9.5"x13" (Front) 26"x13"x13" (Rear)
Brakes: Carbone industrie/AP

Dimensions

Wheelbase: 2817 mm
Track: 1739 mm (Front) / 1617 mm (Rear)
Dry weight: 505 kg
Fuel capacity: 210 litres

Raced all season, from South Africa to Australia.

• **118**_Coming after the Donington fiasco, an impeccable win at Imola did Alain Prost the world of good. He was badly affected by the media frenzy following his drive in England and the Frenchman admitted he was getting tired of all the pressure that was being loaded onto his shoulders. And the season was only just getting underway.

admit it was in the wrong. *"We were very proud of the fact we had a direct line to the weatherman at the nearby airport,"* explains Alain with a smile. *"He said there would be a shower, so when the first drops fell, we changed tyres and then, poof! it was dry again. I hold the record for the number of visits to the pits, seven I think. I guess the only way to deal with it was to treat the situation as a joke."* In fact, at the time, Alain was not laughing at all after this catastrophic race. Ayrton Senna had taken the lead in the championship in his not very special McLaren-Ford. It is worth remembering that on that freezing cold day on the little English circuit, the Brazilian produced one of the most amazing drives of his career. *"We were beaten by Ayrton, who made an incredible start and he kept up a crazy pace for the first three or four laps,"* admits Frank Williams. *"That day, he was really in a class of his own. Alain drove as fast as he could by working his way through the traffic."*

Prost made up for it with two convincing wins in Imola and Barcelona, but the Spanish win saw him in a lot of pain caused by an abnormal vibration and, for the first time in his career, Alain came very close to pulling out because of exhaustion. Once again on pole in the streets of Monaco (his sixth in a row since the start of the season,) he seemed to be setting off for a third win on the trot. Did this made the powers that be think that the Frenchman's impending dominance of the championship was a bad thing? Whatever the reason, he was penalised for a jumped start, while Schumacher and Berger who had committed the same crime were left to get on with it. That meant Prost was 4th, one lap down and very angry. The incredible Ayrton made the most of it to move back into the title lead, which caused a few sour comments from those elements of the media mentioned earlier. The more impartial observers pointed out that Prost invariably took pole (he nailed 13 out of 16 this year!) and that for someone reckoned not to be

● **119_**"Mind if I join in with you young guys?" Alain in full discussion with Michael Schumacher and Damon Hill at Monaco. He remembers his team-mate as someone with whom he formed " a very complimentary tandem. Damon had a lot of experience with the active suspension. He was the driver who had done the most running with the system and he even taught me a thing or two from time to time. Whereas I brought him some of my racing experience."

too keen on qualifying it was not too shabby, even if the car was a great help.

The Frenchman silenced his critics with wins in Canada, France, Great Britain and Germany. In the last two mentioned, his young team-mate, who had not exactly made waves so far, was beginning to demand his slice of the cake. In both cases, Damon led the race from the start only to lose the chance of glory through wretched bad luck in the final laps. For his part, Alain had decided not to try anything dangerous that might compromise his chances in the championship. In response to Frank Williams' criticism that he was too much of a control freak, Alain replied, *"I don't give a damn about the number of wins I get, what I want is to be world champion."* The champion's mind was fixed on this line of thought, but he was not so immune to victory as to prevent him feeling something at reaching the magic

50 Grand Prix wins in England. When he made it 51 at Hockenheim, he was unaware that his personal score would not evolve from then on.

In the summer of 1993, Alain Prost was in a hurry to get everything over and done with. He wanted the title of course, but everything else as well. He could no longer put up with what he saw as the incessant criticism in the media. *"The atmosphere with the technical team was extraordinary, but I was fed up with the press and their nasty and snide remarks. After a while, you ask yourself what's it all about."* He was also finding all the off-track goings-on connected with the sport a bit tedious. After thirteen years in Formula 1, the champion was weary. He still loved the driving more than anything else, but he would rather not go back to the pits and deal with everything going on in there. Alain kept all these thoughts to himself and waited for the right moment to announce something that only a few close friends knew was about to break. His plans were slightly thwarted in Hungary, Belgium and Italy where Damon Hill finally got the upper hand. Each time, the champagne had to be put back on ice and finally it was in Portugal that the corks popped. After a sensible drive behind the leader, Michael Schumacher in his Benetton, who knew that his illustrious pursuer was not about to try anything risky, Alain took the chequered flag in second place to take his fourth world championship title. The Frenchman's fans were happy, but equally sad. That same morning, Alain Prost had officially announced, to everyone's great surprise that he was hanging up his helmet come the end of the season. Alain freed up a place for Ayrton Senna and freed up his spirit at the same time. There were still two rounds remaining in Japan and

Australia. He would tackle them as best he could, without any pressure just to enjoy racing again. He admitted he would really like to win one more time. His old enemy Ayrton would rob him of that final pleasure, winning both races. In both events, Prost was second and everyone watched their reaction on the Suzuka podium. Absolutely nothing new happened and it was in Adelaide, for the very last grand prix of Alain's career that Ayrton turned to him and offered his hand. The two men stared at one another and stood together on the top step of the podium. An era was coming to an end. And in a strange way, it was thus Ayrton Senna who reminded the world who Alain Prost was: one of the greatest champions in the history of the sport, with an amazing track record and immense prestige. He was a champion who had decided with a clear conscience not to race for one year too many. He retired at his peak and in glory. ■

● **120**_Lap of honour at Estoril. Alain had never gone in for the victory flag routine so beloved of Senna. But on this occasion, which would never be repeated, he did not have to be asked twice to grab the blue, white and red and proudly proclaim his identity.

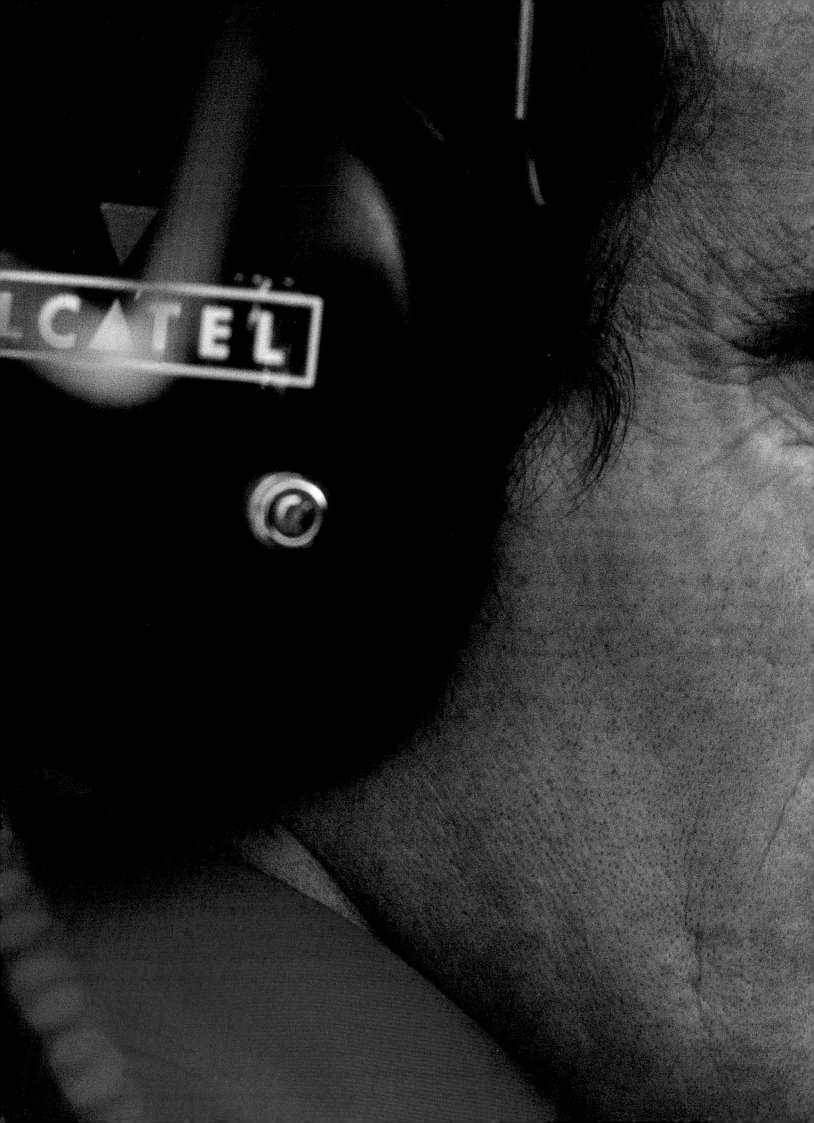

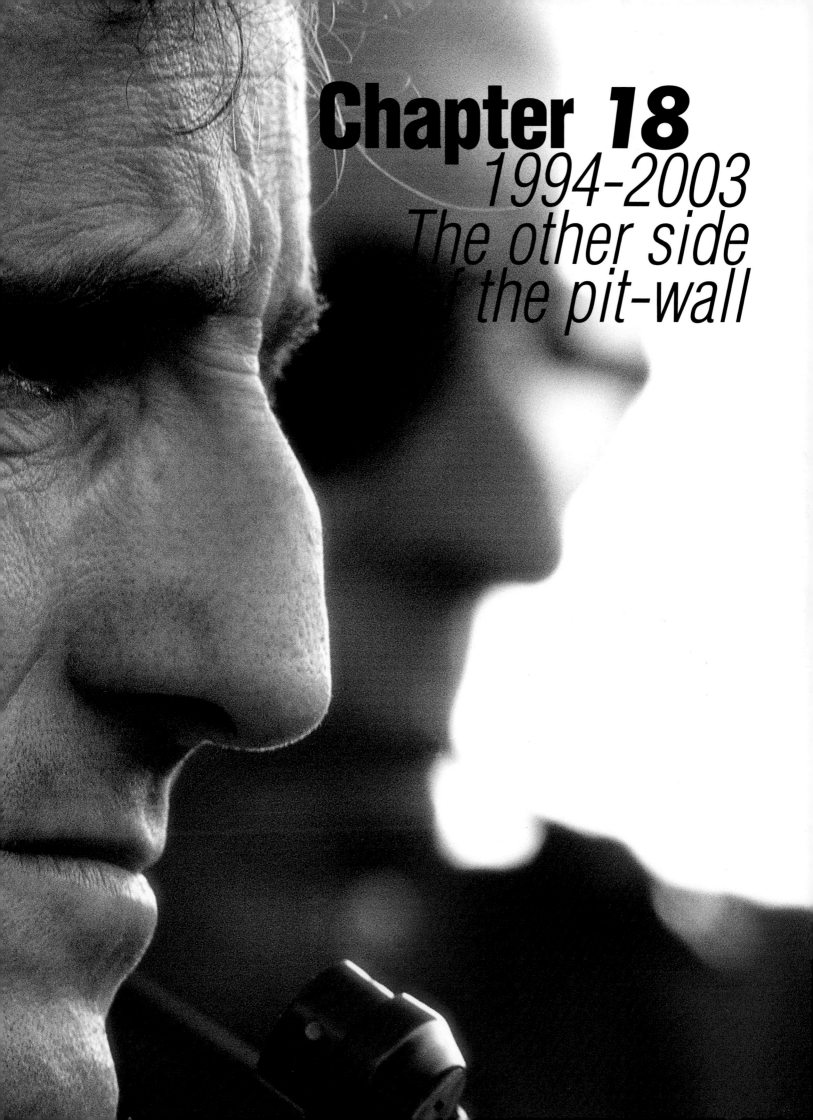

Chapter 18
1994-2003
The other side of the pit-wall

• 122_In 1996, Alain Prost
the consultant immersed
himself fully and with
pleasure into the role of
adviser at McLaren, while
learning from experts at the
same time. *"When I left
McLaren to take over Ligier, it
was a real wrench. Mainly,
because they had been
competitive right from 1997
just as we had expected from
what we had seen in 1996. I
therefore did not reap the
benefit of this success. It was
a tough move to make as I
was happy there and the
atmosphere was
extraordinary."*

He had barely put his helmet down and got out of his race suit after the 1993 Australian Grand Prix before Ron Dennis strode up to him and came right out with it: *"I know why you're going, but you don't really want to go. Come and join me."* Alain Prost listened attentively while the McLaren boss outlined his problems: he had to develop his new car with the brand new Peugeot V10 and Senna was no longer there. Prost refused, but Dennis would not let go and the Frenchman finally gave in and accepted to do a four day test, paid for mind you, at Estoril at the start of 1994. *"From the very first day, I told myself this was stupid. I didn't want to get back into all that and it pissed me off not being competitive against Ayrton in the Williams. At the end of the session, I rang Ron and told him I wouldn't be driving for him. He was so angry he hung up on me!"* Relieved and free now that he had not succumbed to temptation, Prost decided to give himself time to think about his future and returned to the role of commentator for French television. It would give him the chance to talk to the drivers in a relaxed fashion, especially Ayrton Senna. The two men had resumed relations which seemed to be growing stronger. The Brazilian spoke to his new friend of his concerns about his

Williams and the team. Alain was only able to offer advice based on his experience the previous year and wish him good luck for the races. That is how, with twenty minutes to go to the start at Imola, he went to offer a word of encouragement in the back of the team garage. A few hours later, Alain Prost knew beyond doubt that something had changed forever.

During 1994, aside from his broadcasting role, Prost was a high class representative for Renault. Apart from various promotional appearances, he got to drive the famous V10-engined Espace at the Paul Ricard circuit for a few lucky VIPs. As a promotional gambit, Renault had worked with Matra to put a 780 horsepower V10, mated with the sequential gearbox and the entire back end of a Williams into the body of the popular people carrier. It was a one-off styling exercise that was supervised by Gérard Ducarouge. *"It shifted!"* he recalls. *"It weighed 1600 kg, but it was quick enough to drain the colour from its passengers. When they got out they were usually as white as their overalls!"* Despite the financial incentive, Alain began to get bored and his days as an F1 taxi driver did not last long, while the situation with Renault was beginning to lose its

appeal. Amongst other tasks, Prost was asked to put together a proposal for a 100% Renault F1 team. Just as he was getting everything in place and hoping for the green light, the management red-flagged the project. Alain was by now lacking motivation and in any case, another tempting offer appeared over the horizon.

Having divorced from Peugeot during the 1994 season, Ron Dennis had joined forces on a long-term deal with Mercedes. Dennis and the three-pronged star boss Norbert Haug were pushing to have the former champion on board as technical adviser to the team. Prost was soon seduced by the thought of returning to work with people he liked and a more than competent engine supplier. It was now 1995 and the little world of Formula 1 spotted a well known and slightly built silhouette back in the paddock to observe and to test. On several occasions, Alain got behind the wheel of the McLaren-Mercedes to give his opinion on the engine, suggesting improvements to Mario Illien, the designer of the German V10. The Frenchman took pleasure once again at being back on the circuits, while experiencing for the first time the niceties of running a team in a convivial environment which brought back happy memories of the good times

with McLaren. At the end of 1996, all this experience he had gathered would prove very useful. The Ligier team was on the edge of the precipice. The French champion was under pressure from all sides to "do something."

Twice before, Prost had considered starting his own team, during 1989 when the situation within McLaren was beginning to get oppressive, he came up with a plan with help from Elf's François Guiter, Hugues de Chaunac and John Barnard. Even the work load had been agreed: Alain at the wheel, Hugues as sporting director and John as technical director. All they needed was an engine that should have come from Renault. But the motive power proved to be the stumbling block and the project was stillborn. Then, at the start of 1992, there was the Ligier episode, which as have we have seen, never got off the ground. In 1996, it all seemed more serious and better prepared. In fact, all that was needed was the "yes" from Alain and another affirmative from Peugeot group president, Jacques Calvet. Appeals were made to national pride amongst the French politicians who acted as intermediaries and finally, in February 1997, Alain Prost officially became the boss of Prost Grand Prix.

● **123**_Jarno Trulli and Olivier Panis would be the only Prost Grand Prix drivers to provide their boss Alain Prost with the delight of a podium finish: in 1997, Olivier finished 3rd in Brazil and 2nd in Spain, while Jarno was 2nd at the Nurburgring in 1999. Joy was short-lived for Alain as he had to face an ever more disastrous situation as the seasons slipped by.

The Prost Grand Prix saga staggered on for five seasons, up to the start of 2002. At that point, sport was no longer the issue, it was down to judicial decisions as the company went into administration. The factory was closed down, the equipment sold and the staff went their way. It is not the mission of this book to examine the whys and wherefores of how the dream turned into a nightmare and we feel that more time needs to pass by before the tangled web can be unravelled and blame apportioned in what can only be seen as a terrible waste. Personally, Alain Prost came out of this marathon extenuated, bitter and sad. He had wanted to save a national team that was on the road to perdition. He succeeded in delaying its departure and kept the hope alive, because but for his intervention, Ligier would have slipped away at the end of 1996. He wanted to prove everyone in the paddock wrong, especially the British element that said the French were obviously incapable of setting up a Formula 1 team. He failed and, as a proud man aiming at the high and mighty, he suffered.

Long holidays in the sun where no one knows anything about Formula 1 served to get him back in shape mentally and physically; he was once again a man who liked a challenge. At forty seven years of age, Alain Prost had no intention of living without the motivating force of a new project. He was made offers from all over the world and he examined them while taking his time. He wanted above all to feel human again and close to something, feelings that had cruelly escaped him over the past few years. Always curious, always looking for a challenge, Alain was intrigued by the idea of racing on ice, something he knew nothing about. It proved to be the one thing that got him interested enough to get behind the wheel. Max Mammers, a builder of "Silhouette" cars used in the Trophee Andros, held every winter on ice tracks in the Alps and the Massif Central, offered him a run in November 2002 at Val Thorens. Alain thus discovered a world that was the complete antithesis of the one he had know during twenty years of racing on tarmac. *"The driving style is* completely different," he told us. "You have to slide to go quickly, using the torque and also studs for grip. You have to be able to recognise the various different conditions to get the hang of this discipline. There is fresh ice, ice covered with snow and even some corners with a bit of tarmac showing through. You also have to look after the tyres over the course of the weekend as the studs don't last forever. Apart from holding a steering wheel and pressing the pedals, it does not have a single thing in common with an F1 car." Having caught the bug, Alain took part in four events between January and March 2003, at the wheel of an Opel Astra T3F, just to learn the ropes.

In June, Prost was therefore able to lift the lid on his plans. He would drive for Toyota France in the 2003-2004 Trophee Andros at the wheel of a Corolla "Silhouette" specially prepared by the Oreca company owned by his old friend, Hugues de Chaunac. The aim was to get as much experience as possible and win a few races before mounting a serious attack on the 2004-2005 championship. With second place in the championship behind the undisputed maestro, Ivan Muller and three wins, one of them in the second race at the Alpe d'Huez, plus a few podiums, it was a fulfilling experience for the four times Formula 1 world champion. "It's really satisfying to have succeeded with this project and at the same time to have satisfied those involved and the general public. Now I want to do things on a human level. If I am offered other projects I will look at them, but I have nothing planned or programmed. Now, I take things as they come." Alain Prost is serene once again and delivers his own conclusion: "I want to enjoy myself and make others happy." ■

● **125**_In 2003, at the wheel of this Toyota Corolla with a Lexus 340 horsepower 3 litre V6 engine, Alain Prost rediscovered the joy of racing on a terrain he had never experienced before. *"I had never driven a single lap on ice or snow,"* he admitted. Faithful to his reputation, the "Professor" learned quickly thanks to his eternal quest for perfection and he was soon on the pace.
(DPPI)

STATISTICS

Titles won

_KARTING

1973   French Champion, Junior category
         European Champion, Junior category
1974   French Champion, Senior category

_SINGLE SEATERS

1975   "Volant Elf" winner (Paul Ricard)
1976   French Formula Renault Champion
1977   European Formula Renault Champion
1978   French Formula 3 Champion
1979   French and European Formula 3 Champion
1985   Formula 1 World Champion
1986   Formula 1 World Champion
1989   Formula 1 World Champion
1993   Formula 1 World Champion

199 Grands Prix
4 Formule 1 World titles
51 wins, 33 pole positions,
41 fastest race laps

1980_ McLaren M29B/C-Ford from Argentina to Austria
McLaren M30-Ford from Netherlands to United States   Tyres Goodyear

	GRAND PRIX		CIRCUIT	QUALIFYING	RACE	RACE LAP
1.	Argentina	13 Januar	Buenos Aires	12nd (1:46.75)	6th at 1 lap	13th (1:54.13)
2.	Brazil	27 Januar	Interlagos	13rd (2:24.95)	5th at 2:25.41	9th (2:30.88)
3.	South Africa	1st March	Kyalami	22th (1:13.76)	Withdrawn (acc. in qual.)	-
4.	United States West	30 March	Long Beach	Withdrawn	Withdrawn	
5.	Belgium	4 May	Zolder	19th (1:22.26)	Rtd (transmission)	19th (1:24.89)
6.	Monaco	18 May	Monaco	10th (1:26.826)	Rtd (accident)	
7.	Spain*	1st June	Jarama	6th (1:13.631)	Rtd (engine)	18th (1:18.114)
8.	France	29 June	Paul Ricard	7th (1:40.63)	Rtd (transmission)	14th (1:44.87)
9.	Great Britain	13 July	Brands Hatch	7th (1:12.63)	6th at 1 lap	6th (1:14.118)
10.	Germany	10 August	Hockenheim	14th (1:48.75)	11th at 1 lap	7th (1:50.15)
11.	Austria	17 August	Österreichring	12nd (1:34.35)	7th at 1:33.41	11th (1:35.88)
12.	Netherlands	31 August	Zandvoort	18th (1:19.07)	6th at 1:22.62	10th (1:20.77)
13.	Italy	14 September	Imola	24th (1:37.284)	7th at 1 lap	8th (1:37.78)
14.	Canada	28 September	Montréal-Notre Dame	12th (1:29.804)	Rtd (accident/suspension)	5th (1:30.19)
15.	United States	4 October	Watkins Glen	13th (1:35.998)	Withdrawn (acc. in qual.)	-

Position in world championship: 15th / 5 points
Average points per race for season: 0.35

(*) Spain : Event declared non-championship by FISA, following a major disagreement with the Bernie Ecclestone run FOCA.

1981_ Renault RE20B from United States West to San Marino
Renault RE30 from Belgium to Las Vegas   Tyres Michelin

	GRAND PRIX		CIRCUIT	QUALIFYING	RACE	RACE LAP
1.	United States West	15 March	Long Beach	14th (1:20.98)	Rtd (acc. with de Cesaris)	
2.	Brazil	29 March	Rio-Jacarepaguà	5th (1:36.670)	Rtd (acc. with Pironi)	13th (1:57.12)
3.	Argentina	12 April	Buenos Aires	2nd (1:42.981)	3rd at 9.98	4th (1:46.57)
4.	San Marino	3 May	Imola	4th (1:35.579)	Rtd (gearbox)	23rd (1:57.39)
5.	Belgium	17 May	Zolder	12th (1:24.63)	Rtd (clutch)	22nd (1:41.44)
6.	Monaco	31 May	Monaco	9th (1:26.953)	Rtd (engine)	13th (1:29.90)
7.	Spain	21 June	Jarama	5th (1:14.669)	Rtd (accident)	8th (1:18.81)
8.	France	5 July	Dijon-Prenois	3rd (1:06.36)	**1st 1:35:48.13**	FRL (1:09.14)
9.	Great Britain	18 July	Silverstone	2nd (1:11.046)	Rtd (engine)	2nd (1:15.19)
10.	Germany	2 August	Hockenheim	**Pole (1:47.50)**	2nd at 11.52	3rd (1:53.51)
11.	Austria	16 August	Österreichring	2nd (1:32.321)	Rtd (front suspension)	5th (1:38.41)
12.	Netherlands	29 August	Zandvoort	**Pole (1:29.200)**	**1st 1:40:22.43**	3rd (1:22.06)
13.	Italy	13 September	Monza	3rd (1:34.374)	**1st 1:26:33.897**	4th (1:37.702)
14.	Canada	27 September	Montréal-Notre Dame	4th (1:29.908)	Rtd (acc. with Mansell)	6th (1:51.197)
15.	Las Vegas	17 October	Las Vegas	5th (1:18.433)	2nd at 20:048.	4th (1:21.249)

Position in world championship: 5th / 43 points
2 pole positions, 3 wins, 1 fastest race lap
Average points per race for season: 2.86

1982_ Renault RE30B   Tyres Michelin

	GRAND PRIX		CIRCUIT	QUALIFYING	RACE	RACE LAP
1.	South Africa	23 Januar	Kyalami	5th (1:08.133)	**1st 1:32:08.401**	FRL (1:08.278)
2.	Brazil	21 March	Rio-Jacarepaguà	**Pole (1:28.208)**	**1st 1:44:33.134***	3rd (1:37.016)
3.	United States West	4 April	Long Beach	4th (1:27.979)	Rtd (accident/brakes)	14th (1:33.052)
4.	San Marino	25 April	Imola	2nd (1:30.249)	Rtd (engine)	7th (1:37.734)
5.	Belgium	9 May	Zolder	**Pole (1:15.701)**	Rtd (accident)	8th (1:21.223)
6.	Monaco	23 May	Monaco	4th (1:24.439)	Rtd (accident)	2nd (1:26.618)
7.	United States East	6 June	Detroit	**Pole (1:48.537)**	NC	FRL (1:50.438)
8.	Canada	13 June	Montréal-Notre Dame	3rd (1:42.651)	Rtd (engine)	12th (1:31.426)
9.	Netherlands	3 July	Zandvoort	2nd (1:14.660)	Rtd (engine)	6th (1:20.87)
10.	Great Britain	18 July	Brands Hatch	8th (1:10.728)	6th at 41.636	3rd (1:13.264)
11.	France	25 July	Paul Ricard	2nd (1:34.688)	2nd at 17.308	4th (1:42.579)
12.	Germany	8 August	Hockenheim	**Pole (1:48.890)**	Rtd (engine/injection)	4th (1:56.312)
13.	Austria	15 August	Österreichring	3rd (1:28.864)	Rtd (engine/injection)	5th (1:34.457)
14.	Switzerland	29 August	Dijon-Prenois	**Pole (1:01.380)**	2nd at 4.442	FRL (1:07.477)
15.	Italy	12 September	Monza	5th (1:30.026)	Rtd (engine/injection)	2nd (1:33.842)
16.	Las Vegas	25 September	Las Vegas	**Pole (1:16.356)**	4th at 2:08.648	2nd (1:19.924)

Position in world championship: 4th / 34 points
6 pole positions, 2 wins, 3 fastest race laps
Average points per race for season: 2.12

(*) Brazil : 1st after Piquet and Rosberg disqualified.

1983_ Renault RE30C in Brazil
Renault RE40 from United States West to South Africa — Tyres Michelin

	GRAND PRIX		CIRCUIT	QUALIFYING	RACE	RACE LAP
1.	Brazil	13 March	Rio-Jacarepaguà	2nd (1:34.672)	7th at 1 lap	8th (1:42.636)
2.	United States West	27 March	Long Beach	8th (1:28.558)	11th at 3 laps	4th (1:28.717)
3.	France	17 April	Paul Ricard	**Pole (1:36.672)**	**1st 1:34:13.913**	FRL (1:42.695)
4.	San Marino	1st May	Imola	4th (1:32.138)	2nd at 4.442	5th (1:36.833)
5.	Monaco	15 May	Monaco	**Pole (1:24.840)**	3rd at 31.366	2nd (1:27.645)
6.	Belgium	22 May	Spa-Francorchamps	**Pole (2:04.615)**	**1st 1:27:11.502**	2nd (2:07.787)
7.	United States East	5 June	Detroit	13th (1:47.855)	8th at 1 lap	16th (1:50.555)
8.	Canada	12 June	Montréal-Notre Dame	2nd (1:28.830)	5th at 1 lap	4th (1:31.497)
9.	Great Britain	16 July	Silverstone	3rd (1:10.170)	**1st 1:24:39.780**	FRL (1:14.212)
10.	Germany	7 August	Hockenheim	5th (1:51.228)	4th at 2:00.750	4th (1:54.793)
11.	Austria	14 August	Österreichring	5th (1:30.841)	**1st 1:24:32.745**	FRL (1:33.961)
12.	Netherlands	28 August	Zandvoort	4th (1:16.611)	Rtd (acc. with Piquet)	4th (1:20.331)
13.	Italy	11 September	Monza	5th (1:31.144)	Rtd (turbo)	5th (1:34.871)
14.	Europe	25 September	Brands Hatch	8th (1:13.342)	2nd at 6.571	2nd (1:14.616)
15.	South Africa	15 October	Kyalami	5th (1:07.186)	Rtd (turbo)	5th (1:11.166)

Position in world championship: 2nd / 57 points
3 pole positions, 4 wins, 3 fastest race laps
Average points per race for season: 3.8

1984_ McLaren MP4/2-TAG Porsche — Tyres Michelin

	GRAND PRIX		CIRCUIT	QUALIFYING	RACE	RACE LAP
1.	Brazil	25 March	Rio-Jacarepaguà	4th (1:29.330)	**1st 1:42:34.492**	FRL (1:36.499)
2.	South Africa	7 April	Kyalami	5th (1:05.354)	2nd at 1:05.950	2nd (1:08.961)
3.	Belgium	29 April	Zolder	8th (1:16.587)	Rtd (distributor)	18th (1:22.879)
4.	San Marino	6 May	Imola	2nd (1:28.628)	**1st 1:36:53.679**	3rd (1:33.580)
5.	France	20 May	Dijon-Prenois	5th (1:02.982)	7nd at 1 lap	FRL (1:05.257)
6.	Monaco	3 June	Monaco	**Pole (1:22.661)**	**1st 1:01:07.740**	7th (1:55.596)
7.	Canada	17 June	Montréal-Notre Dame	2nd (1:26.198)	3rd at 1:28.320	3rd (1:29.433)
8.	United States	24 June	Detroit	2nd (1:41.640)	5th at 1:55.258	7th (1:47.074)
9.	Dallas	8 July	Dallas	7th (1:38.544)	Rtd (accident)	5th (1:45.976)
10.	Great Britain	27 July	Brands Hatch	2nd (1:11.076)	Rtd (gearbox)	4th (1:13.979)
11.	Germany	5 August	Hockenheim	**Pole (1:47.012)**	**1st 1:24:43.210**	FRL (1:53.538)
12.	Austria	19 August	Österreichring	2nd (1:26.203)	Rtd (spin)	4th (1:33.081)
13.	Netherlands	26 August	Zandvoort	**Pole (1:13.567)**	**1st 1:37:21.468**	2nd (1:20.063)
14.	Italy	9 September	Monza	2nd (1:26.671)	Rtd (engine)	16th (1:35.604)
15.	Europe	7 October	Nürburgring	2nd (1:19.175)	**1st 1:35:13.284**	6th (1:24.182)
16.	Portugal	21 October	Estoril	2nd (1:21.703)	**1st 1:41:11.753**	2nd (1:23.452)

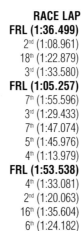

Position in world championship: 2nd / 71,5 points
3 pole positions, 7 wins, 3 fastest race laps
Average points per race for season: 4.46

1985_ McLaren MP4/2B-TAG Porsche — Tyres Goodyear

	GRAND PRIX		CIRCUIT	QUALIFYING	RACE	RACE LAP
1.	Brazil	7 April	Rio-Jacarepaguà	5th (1:29.117)	**1st 1:41:26.115**	FRL (1:36.702)
2.	Portugal	21 April	Estoril	2nd (1:21.420)	Rtd (accident)	3rd (1:44.901)
3.	San Marino	5 May	Imola	6th (1:28.099)	Disqualified*	5th (1:31.549)
4.	Monaco	19 May	Monaco	5th (1:20.885)	**1st 1:51:58.034**	2nd (1:23.898)
5.	Canada	16 June	Montréal-Notre Dame	5th (1:25.557)	3rd at 4.341	6th (1:28.755)
6.	United States	23 June	Detroit	4th (1:44.088)	Rtd (accident/brakes)	12th (1:49.001)
7.	France	7 July	Paul-Ricard	4th (1:33.335)	3rd at 9.285	7th (1:41.991)
8.	Great Britain	21 July	Silverstone	3rd (1:06.308)	**1st 1:18:10.436**	FRL (1:09.886)
9.	Germany	4 August	Hockenheim	3rd (1:18.725)	2nd at 11.661	4th (1:23.810)
10.	Austria	18 August	Österreichring	**Pole (1:25.490)**	**1st 1:20:12.583**	FRL (1:29.241)
11.	Netherlands	25 August	Zandvoort	3rd (1:11.801)	2nd at 0.232	FRL (1:16.538)
12.	Italy	8 September	Monza	5th (1:25.790)	**1st 1:17:59.451**	3rd (1:29.714)
13.	Belgium	15 September	Spa-Francorchamps	**Pole (1:55.306)**	3rd at 56.109	FRL (2:01.730)
14.	Europe	6 October	Brands Hatch	6th (1:09.429)	4th at 1:06.121	2nd (1:11.526)
15.	South Africa	19 October	Kyalami	9th (1:04.376)	3rd at 1:52.794	3rd (1:08.713)
16.	Australia	3 November	Adelaïde	4th (1:21.889)	Rtd (engine)	7th (1:25.388)

Position in world championship:
World Champion / 73 points
2 pole positions, 5 wins, 5 fastest race laps
Average points per race for season: 4.56

(*) San Marino: Prost finishes first, but disqualified for being underweight.

1986 _ McLaren MP4/2C-TAG Porsche — Tyres Goodyear

GRAND PRIX		CIRCUIT	QUALIFYING	RACE	RACE LAP
1. Brazil	23 March	Rio-Jacarepaguà	9th (1:28.099)	Rtd (engine)	6th (1:35.381)
2. Spain	13 April	Jerez	4th (1:22.886)	3rd at 21.492	5th (1:28.497)
3. San Marino	27 April	Imola	4th (1:26.176)	**1st 1:32:28.408**	3rd (1:29.464)
4. Monaco	19 May	Monaco	**Pole (1:22.627)**	**1st 1:55:41.060**	**FRL (1:26.607)**
5. Belgium	25 May	Spa-Francorchamps	3rd (1:54.501)	6th at 2:17.772	**FRL (1:59.282)**
6. Canada	15 June	Montréal-Notre Dame	4th (1:25.192)	2nd at 20.659	3rd (1:26.859)
7. United States	22 June	Detroit	7th (1:40.715)	3rd at 20.824	5th (1:43.293)
8. France	6 July	Paul-Ricard	5th (1:07.266)	2nd at 17.128	4th (1:10.859)
9. Great Britain	13 July	Brands Hatch	6th (1:09.334)	3rd at 1 lap	3rd (1:10.827)
10. Germany	27 July	Hockenheim	2nd (1:42.166)	6th (ran out of fuel)	6th (1:49.649)
11. Hungary	10 August	Hungaroring	3rd (1:29.945)	Rtd (acc. with Arnoux)	5th (1:33.422)
12. Austria	17 August	Österreichring	5th (1:24.346)	**1st 1:21:22.531**	2nd (1:30.751)
13. Italy	7 September	Monza	2nd (1:24.514)	Disqualified*	7th (1:29.501)
14. Portugal	21 September	Estoril	3rd (1:17.710)	2nd at 18.772	2nd (1:21.092)
15. Mexico	12 October	Mexico	6th (1:18.421)	2nd at 25.438	5th (1:20.357)
16. Australia	26 October	Adelaïde	4th (1:19.654)	**1st 1:54:20.388**	2nd (1:20.979)

(*) Italy : Prost changes cars before the start after the green flag.

Position in world championship:
World Champion / 72 points
1 pole position, 4 wins, 2 fastest race laps
Average points per race for season: 4.5

1987 _ McLaren MP4/3-TAG Porsche — Tyres Goodyear

GRAND PRIX		CIRCUIT	QUALIFYING	RACE	RACE LAP
1. Brazil	12 April	Rio-Jacarepaguà	5th (1:29.175)	**1st 1:39:45.141**	9th (1:35.881)
2. San Marino	3 May	Imola	3rd (1:26.135)	Rtd (alternator belt)	7th (1:31.409)
3. Belgium	17 May	Spa-Francorchamps	6th (1:54.186)	**1st 1:27:03.217**	**FRL (1:57.153)**
4. Monaco	31 May	Monaco	4th (1:25.083)	Rtd (engine)	4th (1:28.891)
5. United States	21 June	Detroit	5th (1:42.357)	3rd at 33.327	4th (1:41.340)
6. France	5 July	Paul-Ricard	2nd (1:06.877)	3rd at 55.255	3rd (1:11.324)
7. Great Britain	12 July	Silverstone	4th (1:08.577)	Rtd (clutch/electrical)	5th (1:13.346)
8. Germany	26 July	Hockenheim	3rd (1:43.202)	Rtd/7th (alternator belt)	2nd (1:46.807)
9. Hungary	9 August	Hungaroring	4th (1:30.156)	3rd at 1:27.456	3rd (1:31.602)
10. Austria	16 August	Österreichring	9th (1:26.170)	6th at 2 laps	5th (1:29.291)
11. Italy	6 September	Monza	5th (1:24.946)	15th at 4 laps	3rd (1:26.882)
12. Portugal	20 September	Estoril	3rd (1:17.994)	**1st 1:37:03.906**	2nd (1:19.509)
13. Spain	27 September	Jerez	7th (1:24.596)	2nd at 22.225	4th (1:27.459)
14. Mexico	18 October	Mexico	5th (1:18.742)	Rtd (acc. with Piquet)	**FRL (1:43.844)**
15. Japan	1st November	Suzuka	2nd (1:40.652)	7th at 1 lap	4th (1:21.381)
16. Australia	15 November	Adelaïde	2nd (1:17.967)	Rtd (brakes)	-

Position in world championship: 4th / 46 points
3 wins, 2 fastest race laps
Average points per race for season: 2.875

1988 _ McLaren MP4/4-Honda — Tyres Goodyear

GRAND PRIX		CIRCUIT	QUALIFYING	RACE	RACE LAP
1. Brazil	3 April	Rio-Jacarepaguà	3rd (1:28.782)	**1st 1:36:06.857**	3rd (1:33.540)
2. San Marino	1st May	Imola	2nd (1:27.919)	2nd at 2.304	**FRL (1:29.685)**
3. Monaco	15 May	Monaco	2nd (1:25.425)	**1st 1:57:17.077**	2nd (1:26.714)
4. Mexico	29 May	Mexico	2nd (1:18.097)	**1st 1:30:15.737**	**FRL (1:18.608)**
5. Canada	12 June	Montréal-Notre Dame	2nd (1:21.863)	2nd at 5.934	2nd (1:25.045)
6. United States	19 June	Detroit	4th (1:42.019)	2nd at 38.713	**FRL (1:44.836)**
7. France	3 July	Paul-Ricard	**Pole (1:07.589)**	**1st 1:37:37.328**	**FRL (1:11.737)**
8. Great Britain	10 July	Silverstone	4th (1:10.736)	Rtd (handling)	22nd (1:27.456)
9. Germany	24 July	Hockenheim	2nd (1:44.873)	2nd at 13.609	2nd (2:04.888)
10. Hungary	7 August	Hungaroring	7th (1:28.778)	2nd at 0.529	**FRL (1:30.639)**
11. Belgium	28 August	Spa-Francorchamps	2nd (1:54.128)	2nd at 30.470	3rd (2:01.702)
12. Italy	11 September	Monza	2nd (1:26.277)	Rtd (engine)	4th (1:29.642)
13. Portugal	25 September	Estoril	**Pole (1:17.411)**	**1st 1:37:40.958**	3rd (1:22.063)
14. Spain	2 October	Jerez	2nd (1:24.134)	**1st 1:48:43.851**	**FRL (1:27.847)**
15. Japan	30 October	Suzuka	2nd (1:42.177)	2nd at 13.363	2nd (1:46.482)
16. Australia	13 November	Adelaïde	2nd (1:17.880)	**1st 1:53:14.676**	**FRL (1:21.216)**

Position in world championship: 2nd / 87 points
2 pole positions, 7 wins, 7 fastest race laps
Average points per race for season: 5.437

1989_ McLaren MP4/5-Honda

Tyres Goodyear

GRAND PRIX		CIRCUIT	QUALIFYING	RACE	RACE LAP
1. Brazil	26 March	Rio-Jacarepaguà	5th (1:26.620)	2nd at 7.809	11th (1:35.341)
2. San Marino	23 April	Imola	2nd (1:26.235)	2nd at 40.225	FRL (1:26.795)
3. Monaco	7 May	Monaco	2nd (1:23.456)	2nd at 52.529	FRL (1:25.501)
4. Mexico	28 May	Mexico	2nd (1:18.773)	5th at 56.113	2nd (1:20.506)
5. United States	4 June	Phoenix	2nd (1:31.517)	1st 2:01:33.133	2nd (1:34.957)
6. Canada	18 June	Montréal-Notre Dame	Pole (1:20.973)	Rtd (suspension)	21st (1:41.751)
7. France	9 July	Paul-Ricard	Pole (1:07.203)	1st 1:38:29.411	3rd (1:12.500)
8. Great Britain	16 July	Silverstone	2nd (1:09.266)	1st 1:19:22.131	2nd (1:12.193)
9. Germany	30 July	Hockenheim	2nd (1:43.295)	2nd at 18.151	2nd (1:45.977)
10. Hungary	13 August	Hungaroring	5th (1:21.076)	4th at 44.177	2nd (1:22.654)
11. Belgium	27 August	Spa-Francorchamps	2nd (1:51.463)	2nd at 1.304	FRL (2:11.571)
12. Italy	10 September	Monza	4th (1:25.510)	1st 1:19:27.550	FRL (1:28.107)
13. Portugal	24 September	Estoril	4th (1:16.204)	2nd at 32.637	3rd (1:19.385)
14. Spain	1st October	Jerez	3rd (1:21.368)	3rd at 53.788	7th (1:26.758)
15. Japan	22 October	Suzuka	2nd (1:39.771)	Rtd (acc. with Senna)	2nd (1:43.506)
16. Australia	5 November	Adelaïde	2nd (1:17.403)	Rtd (refuses to race)	-

Position in world championship:
World Champion / 76 points
2 pole positions, 4 wins, 4 fastest race laps
Average points per race for season: 4.75

1990_ Ferrari 641

Tyres Goodyear

GRAND PRIX		CIRCUIT	QUALIFYING	RACE	RACE LAP
1. United States	11 March	Phoenix	7th (1:29.910)	Rtd (gearbox)	13th (1:33.170)
2. Brazil	25 March	Interlagos	5th (1:18.631)	1st 1:37:21.258	2nd (1:20.010)
3. San Marino	13 May	Imola	6th (1:25.179)	4th at 6.843	2nd (1:27.164)
4. Monaco	27 May	Monaco	2nd (1:21.776)	Rtd (electronical)	5th (1:25.888)
5. Canada	10 June	Montréal-Notre Dame	3rd (1:20.826)	5th at 15.820	4th (1:23.078)
6. Mexico	24 June	Mexico	13th (1:17.670)	1st 1:32:35.783	FRL (1:17.958)
7. France	8 July	Paul-Ricard	4th (1:04.781)	1st 1:33:29.606	3rd (1:08.212)
8. Great Britain	15 July	Silverstone	5th (1:08.336)	1st 1:18:30.999	2nd (1:11.526)
9. Germany	29 July	Hockenheim	3rd (1:41.732)	4th at 45.270	5th (1:46.839)
10. Hungary	12 August	Hungaroring	8th (1:19.029)	Rtd (gearbox)	14th (1:24.214)
11. Belgium	26 August	Spa-Francorchamps	3rd (1:51.043)	2nd at 3.550	FRL (1:55.087)
12. Italy	9 September	Monza	2nd (1:22.935)	2nd at 6.054	2nd (1:26.254)
13. Portugal	23 September	Estoril	2nd (1:13.595)	3rd at 4.189	3rd (1:18.396)
14. Spain	30 September	Jerez	2nd (1:18.824)	1st 1:48:01.461	3rd (1:25.177)
15. Japan	21 October	Suzuka	2nd (1:37.228)	Rtd (acc. with Senna)	—
16. Australia	4 November	Adelaïde	4th (1:16.365)	3rd at 37.259	4th (1:19.434)

Position in world championship: 2nd / 71 points
5 wins, 2 fastest race laps
Average points per race for season: 4.437

1991_ Ferrari 642 from United States to Mexico
Ferrari 643 from France to Japan

Tyres Goodyear

GRAND PRIX		CIRCUIT	QUALIFYING	RACE	RACE LAP
1. United States	10 March	Phoenix	2nd (1:22.255)	2nd at 16.322	2nd (1:26.845)
2. Brazil	24 March	Interlagos	6th (1:17.739)	4th at 19.369	2nd (1:20.635)
3. San Marino	28 April	Imola	3rd (1:22.195)	Not started (Acc. Parade Lap)	FRL (1:24.368)
4. Monaco	12 May	Monaco	7th (1:21.455)	5th at 1 lap	7th (1:24.186)
5. Canada	2 June	Montréal-Notre Dame	4th (1:20.656)	Rtd (gearbox)	19th (1:21.266)
6. Mexico	16 June	Mexico	7th (1:18.183)	Rtd (alternator)	2nd (1:19.144)
7. France	7 July	Magny-Cours	2nd (1:14.789)	2nd at 2.991	2nd (1:26.589)
8. Great Britain	14 July	Silverstone	5th (1:22.478)	3rd at 1:00.150	4th (1:44.059)
9. Germany	28 July	Hockenheim	5th (1:39.034)	Rtd (off)	7th (1:23.305)
10. Hungary	11 August	Hungaroring	4th (1:17.690)	Rtd (engine)	23rd (2:01.161)
11. Belgium	25 August	Spa-Francorchamps	2nd (1:48.821)	Rtd (oil leak)	4th (1:27.153)
12. Italy	8 September	Monza	5th (1:21.825)	3rd at 16.829	10th (1:19.531)
13. Portugal	22 September	Estoril	5th (1:14.352)	Rtd (engine)	4th (1:23.729)
14. Spain	29 September	Barcelona-Cataluña	6th (1:19.936)	2nd at 11.331	6th (1:43.712)
15. Japan	20 October	Suzuka	4th (1:36.670)	4th at 1:20.731	—
16. Australia	3 November	Adelaïde	Absent/fired	-	

Position in world championship: 5th / 34 points
1 fastest race lap
Average points per race for season: 2.125

1993 _ Williams FW15-Renault

Tyres Goodyear

	GRAND PRIX		CIRCUIT	QUALIFYING	RACE	RACE LAP
1.	South Africa	14 March	Kyalami	**Pole (1:15.696)**	**1st 1:38:45.082**	**FRL (1:19.492)**
2.	Brazil	28 March	Interlagos	**Pole (1:15.866)**	Rtd (accident)	5th (1:21.780)
3.	Europe	11 April	Donington Park	**Pole (1:10.458)**	3rd at 1 lap	3rd (1:19.756)
4.	San Marino	25 April	Imola	**Pole (1:22.070)**	**1st 1:33:20.413**	**FRL (1:26.128)**
5.	Spain	9 May	Barcelona-Cataluña	**Pole (1:18.346)**	**1st 1:32:27.685**	4th (1:22.923)
6.	Monaco	23 May	Monaco	**Pole (1:20.557)**	4th at 1 lap	**FRL (1:23.604)**
7.	Canada	13 June	Montréal-Notre Dame	**Pole (1:18.987)**	**1st 1:36:41.822**	2nd (1:21.613)
8.	France	4 July	Magny-Cours	2nd (1:14.524)	**1st 1:38:35.241**	4th (1:20.530)
9.	Great Britain	11 July	Silverstone	**Pole (1:19.006)**	**1st 1:25:38.189**	2nd (1:22.534)
10.	Germany	25 July	Hockenheim	**Pole (1:38.748)**	**1st 1:18:40.885**	3rd (1:42.213)
11.	Hungary	15 August	Hungaroring	**Pole (1:14.631)**	12th at 7 laps	**FRL (1:19.633)**
12.	Belgium	29 August	Spa-Francorchamps	**Pole (1:47.571)**	3rd at 14.988	**FRL (1:51.095)**
13.	Italy	12 September	Monza	**Pole (1:21.179)**	12th at 5 laps	2nd (1:24.407)
14.	Portugal	26 September	Estoril	2nd (1:11.683)	2nd at 0.982	2nd (1:15.780)
15.	Japan	24 October	Suzuka	**Pole (1:37.154)**	2nd at 11.435	**FRL (1:41.176)**
16.	Australia	7 November	Adelaïde	2nd (1:13.807)	2nd at 9.259	2nd (1:15.434)

Position in world championship:
World Champion / 99 points.
13 pole positions, 7 wins, 6 fastest race laps
Average points per race for season: 6.187

INDEX

_ACKNOWLEDGEMENTS

The authors would particularly like to thank Alain Prost for his extensive cooperation.

And for their precious eye-witness accounts and other help: Willy Arnault, John Barnard, Anne Boisnard, Etienne Bruet, Patrick Camus, Hugues de Chaunac, Christian Courtel, Jean-Michel Desnoues, Joseph Dimier, Gérard Ducarouge, Bernard Dudot, Pierre Dupasquier, Michel Fabre, Cesare Fiorio, Jean-Pierre Gauthier, François Guiter, Niki Lauda, Nicola Materazzi, Steve Nichols, Virginie Papin, Antoine Raffaelli, Johnny Rives, Clare Robertson (TAG McLaren media services), Serena Santolamazza (Renault-Sport), Paul Roussel (L'EQUIPE), Clair Vann, John Watson, Frank Williams, Jonathan Williams (Williams sponsorship&marketing services) and lastly the documentation service of the Saint-Chamond town hall.

Some key players in Alain Prost's career declined to answer our questions and we can but respect their decision.

_BIOGRAPHY

"Champion du monde"
Alain Prost with Jean-Louis Moncet – Ed. Carrere-Lafon

"Alain Prost, sur la piste d'une étoile"
Lionel Froissart – Ed. Glénat

"Formule Renault, de la Formule France au Turbo"
Christian Courtel – Ed. du Palmier

"Renault F1 – Les années turbo"
Bernard Dudot, Gérard Larrousse and Jean-Louis Moncet – Ed.

"Autocourse" and "The Formula 1 Yearbook"

"Auto-Hebdo" and "Sport-Auto" magazines

L'EQUIPE newspaper